THIS BOOK BELONGS TO

____

____

DATE

____

Sade Coloring Book

Illustrated by Andre Hollingsworth

Edited by Menia Buckner, treadswell@gmail.com

ISBN 978-1-7352177-0-3

If you are using a marker please place a blank piece of paper behind the coloring pages to prevent bleed-though.

Connect with Andre Hollingsworth online at:

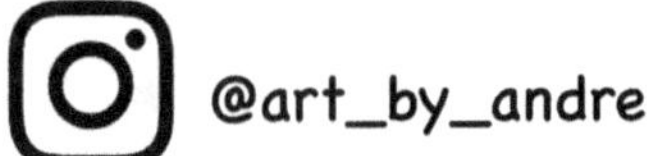

Art By Andre Hollingsworth

For information about custom editions or corporate purchases, please contact Andre at artbyandremn@gmail.com

Made in the USA

Published By: Holli Rock, LLC

I watched the music video for Sade's "The Sweetest Taboo" for the first time on BET. Her sultry contralto was unlike anything I had heard before. Even as a young boy, I was mesmerized by her distinctive beauty: the gold hoop earrings, the bright red lipstick, and her long, black ponytail. I purchased my first Sade album, "Love Deluxe," in high school, and listened to it on my CD player every night.

Over thirty years later, I still adore Sade's music, and have waited impatiently for each of her albums to drop. Her timeless sound inspires me to be creative in my own artistry. Songs like "When am I Gonna Make a Living" encourage me to push through the most challenging moments in life.

For the best experience, play your favorite Sade songs while you color.

Thank you,

Andre Hollingsworth

Helen Folasade Adu was born to a British mother and Nigerian father in Ibadan, Nigeria. She moved to London at the age of four. After finishing school, she designed men's fashion and worked briefly as a model. One night at a party, a friend asked her if she would like to try out as a singer for a band.

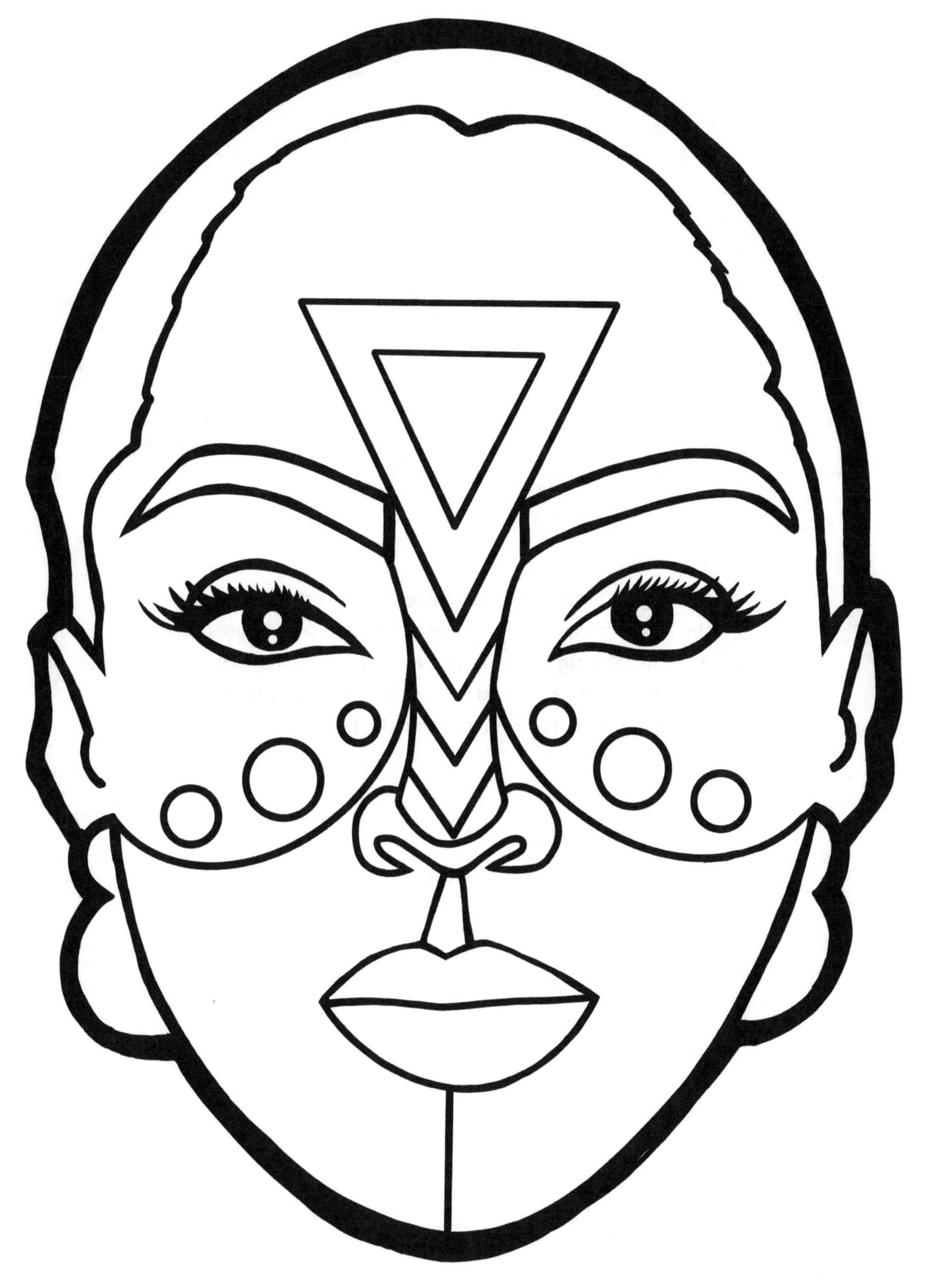

Sade began singing backup in a local band called Pride. She was soon singled out by record companies, but the labels were not interested in the rest of Pride. She signed with Epic Records and took with her bassist Paul Denman, keyboardist Andrew Hale, and saxophonist Stuart Matthewman to form the band Sade.

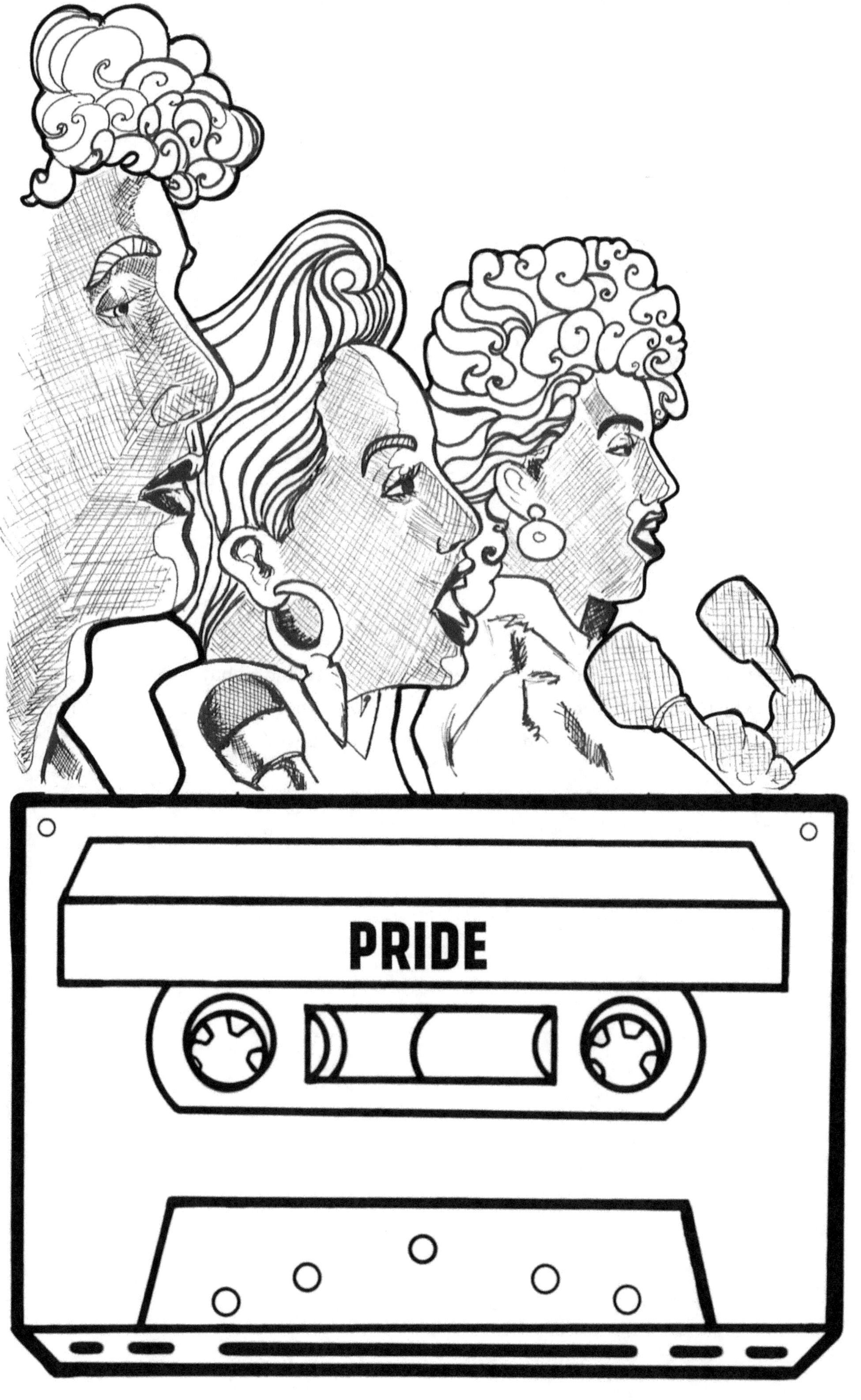
PRIDE

Sade rose to fame in 1984 with her best-selling debut Diamond Life, which was fueled by the hit singles "Smooth Operator," "Your Love is King," and "Hang On to Your Love."

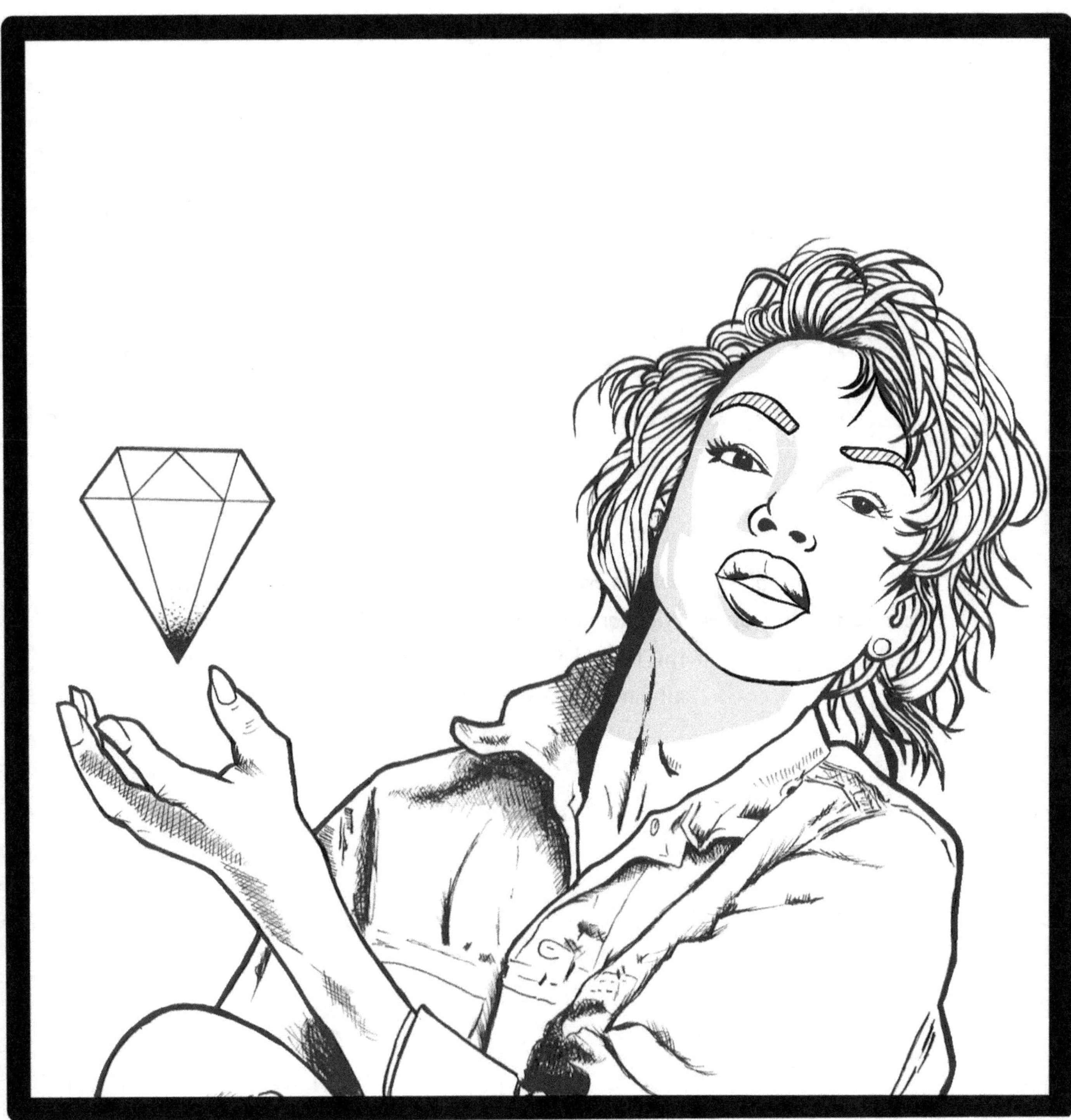

"Your Love is King" was written by Sade and Stuart Matthewman. It was released in the United Kingdom on February 25, 1984 as the album's lead single and in the United States on June 22, 1985 as the album's third U.S. single.

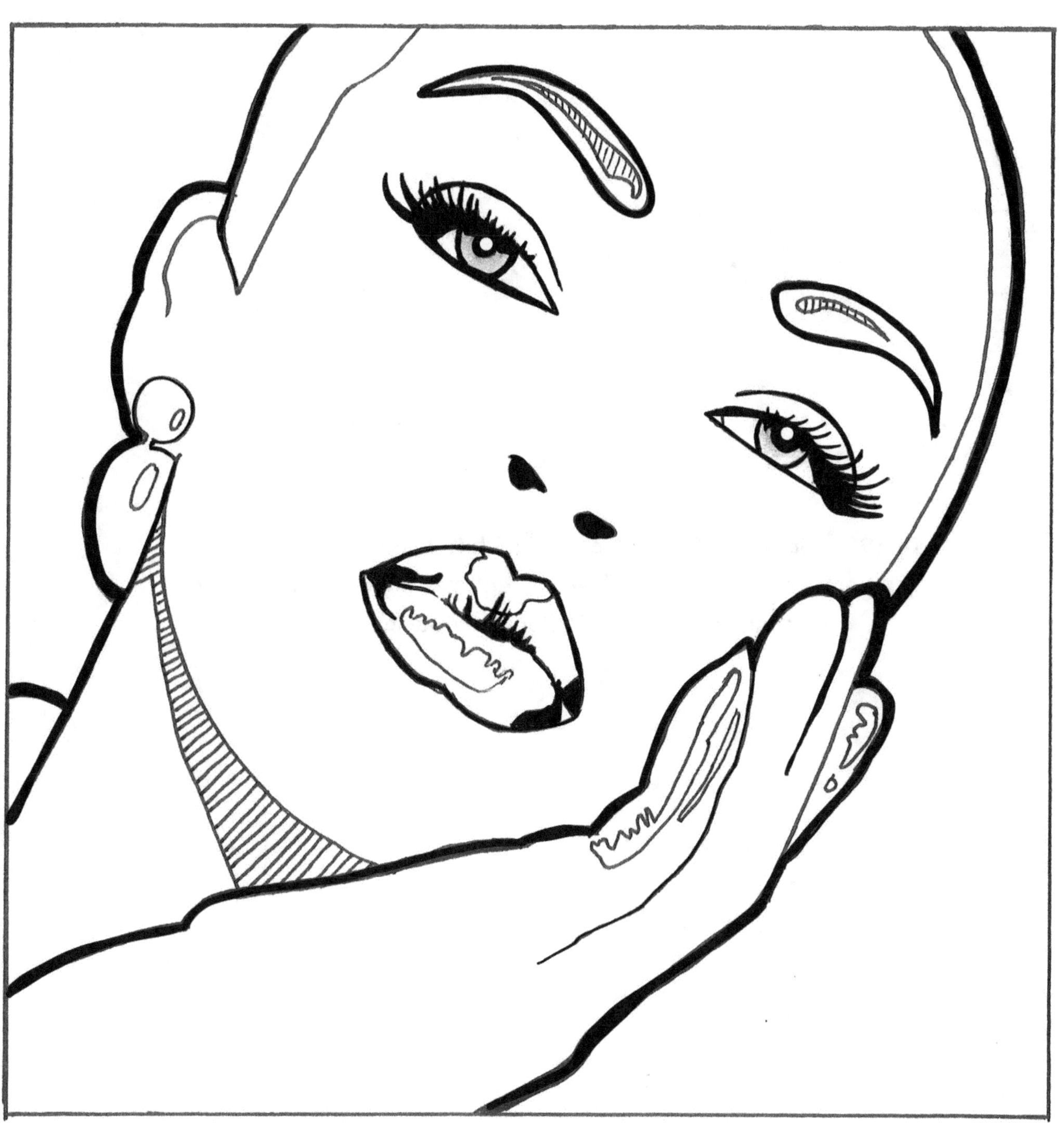

In 1986, Sade released a black and white music video for "Never as Good as the First Time," which features Sade riding a horse through the town of El Rocio in Andalusia, Spain.

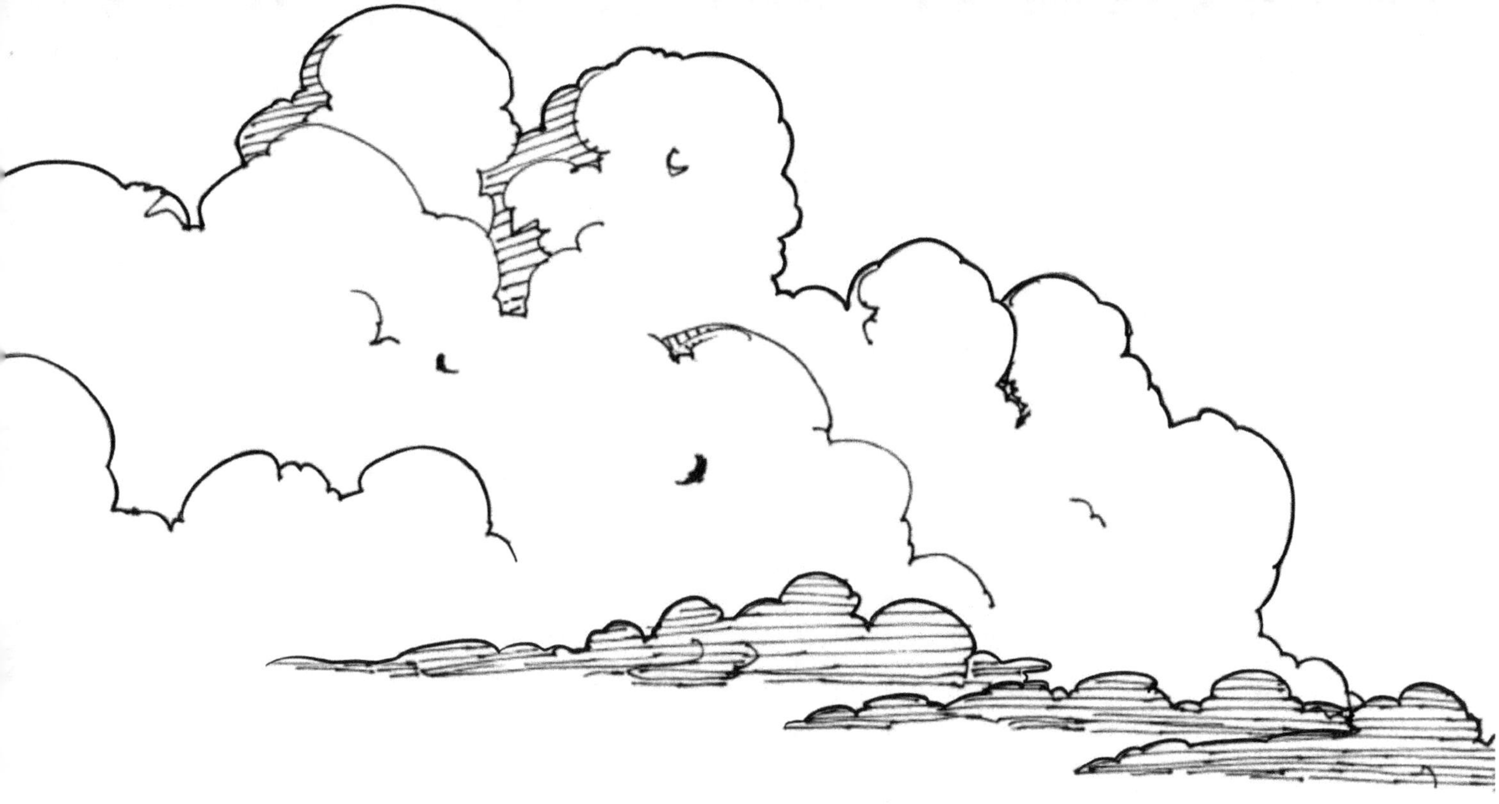

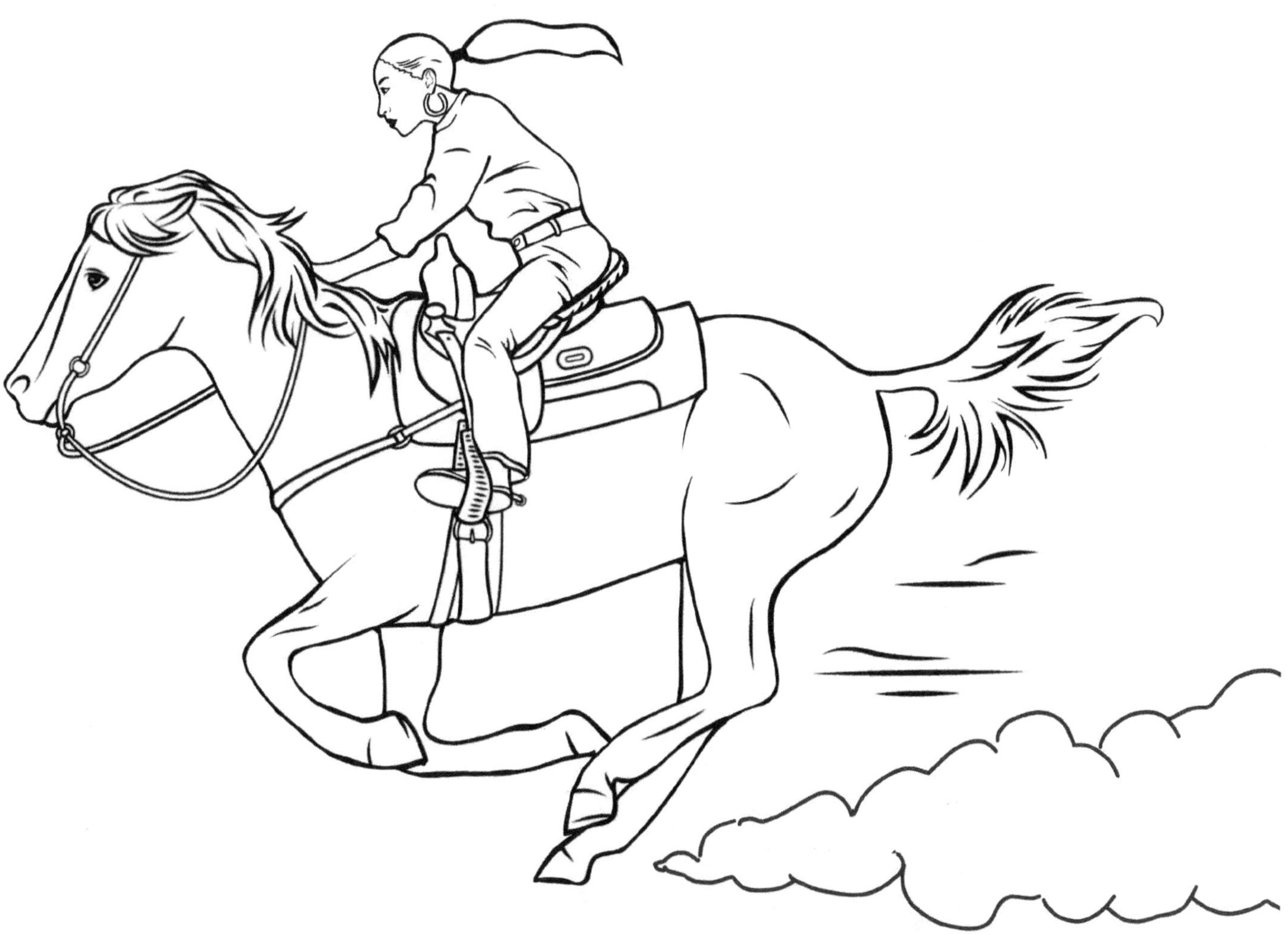

In 1986, Sade was recognized with a Grammy Award
for Best New Artist.

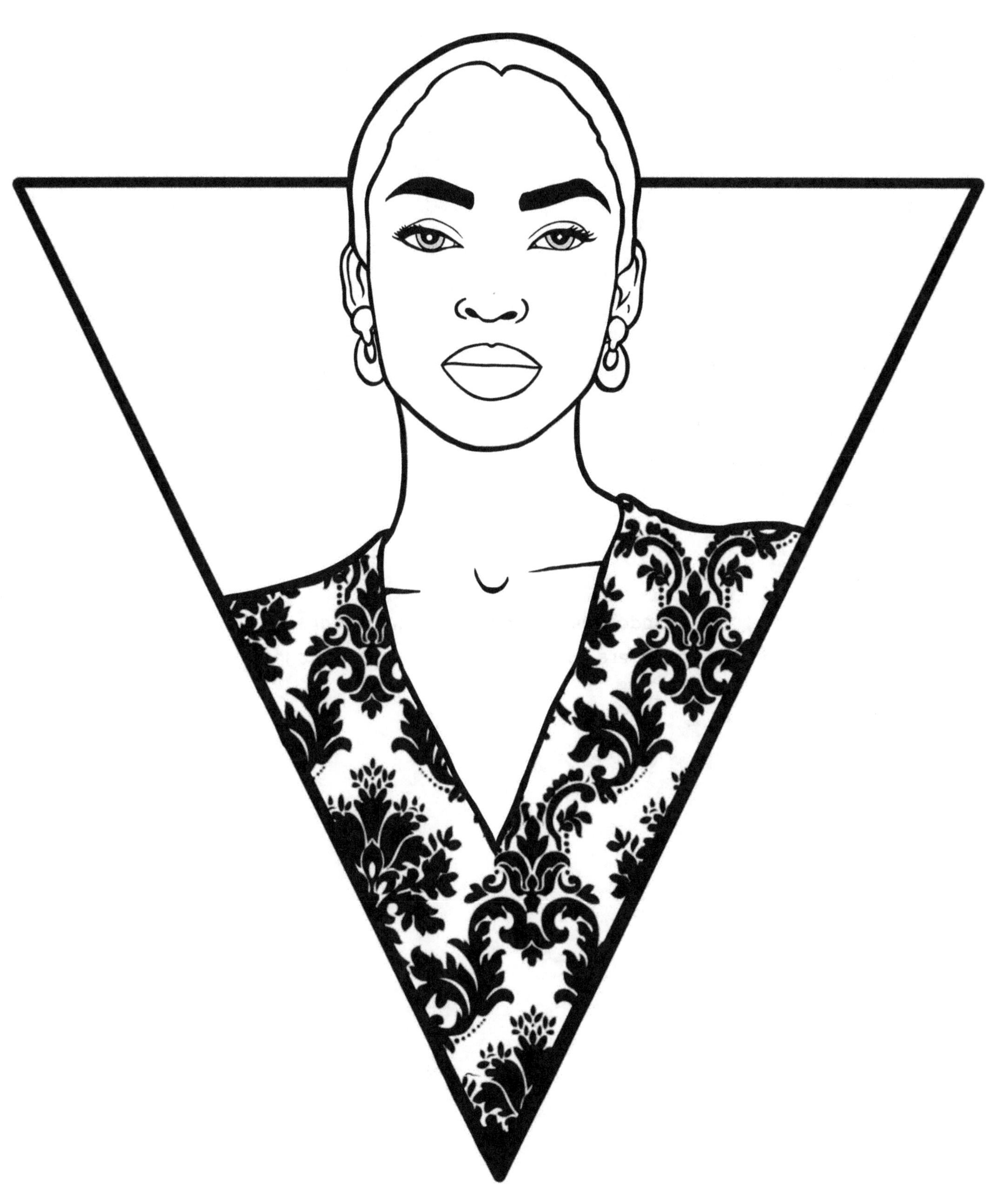

Sade's middle name, Folasade, means
"honor confers your crown" in the Yoruea language.

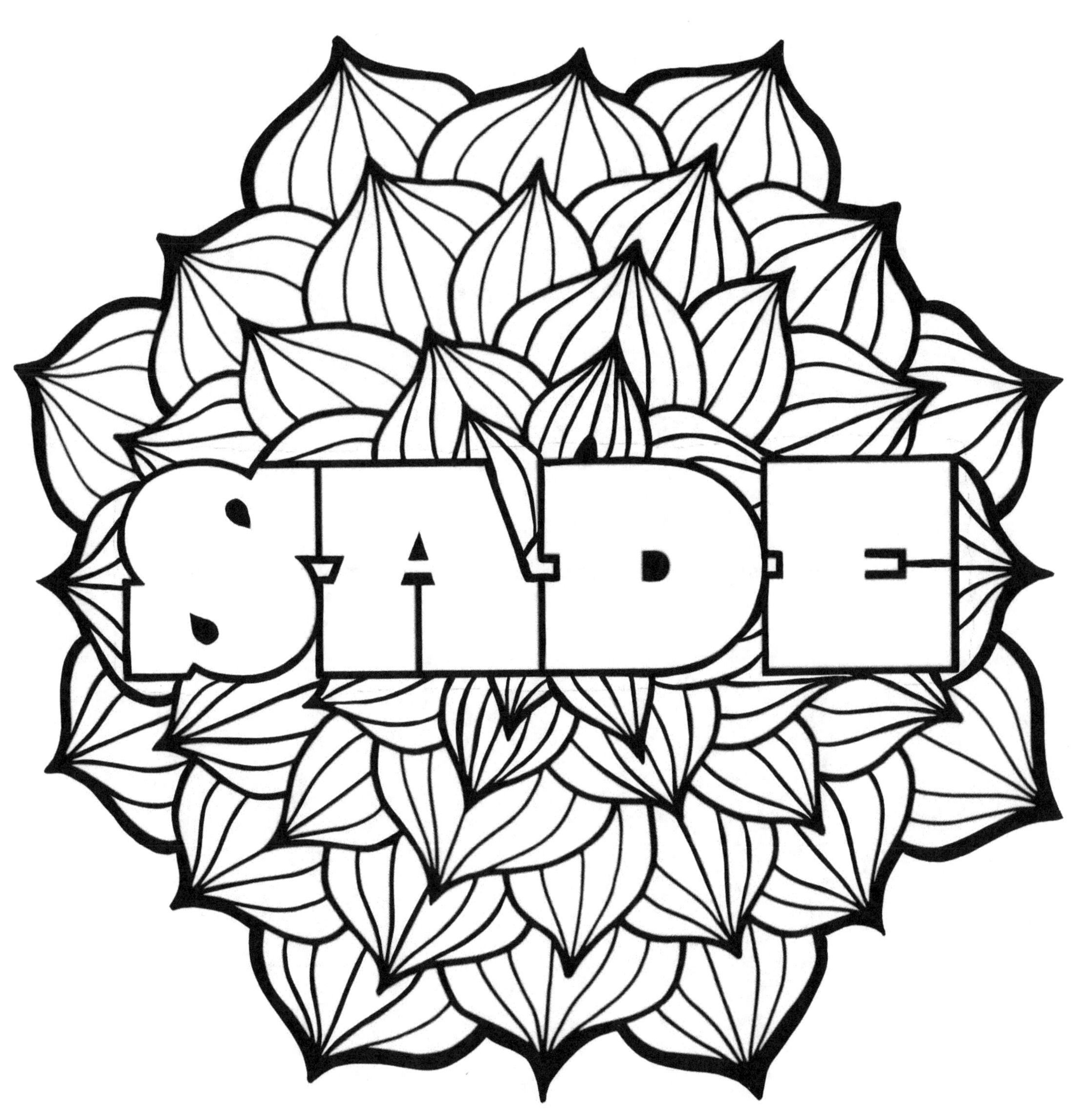
SADE

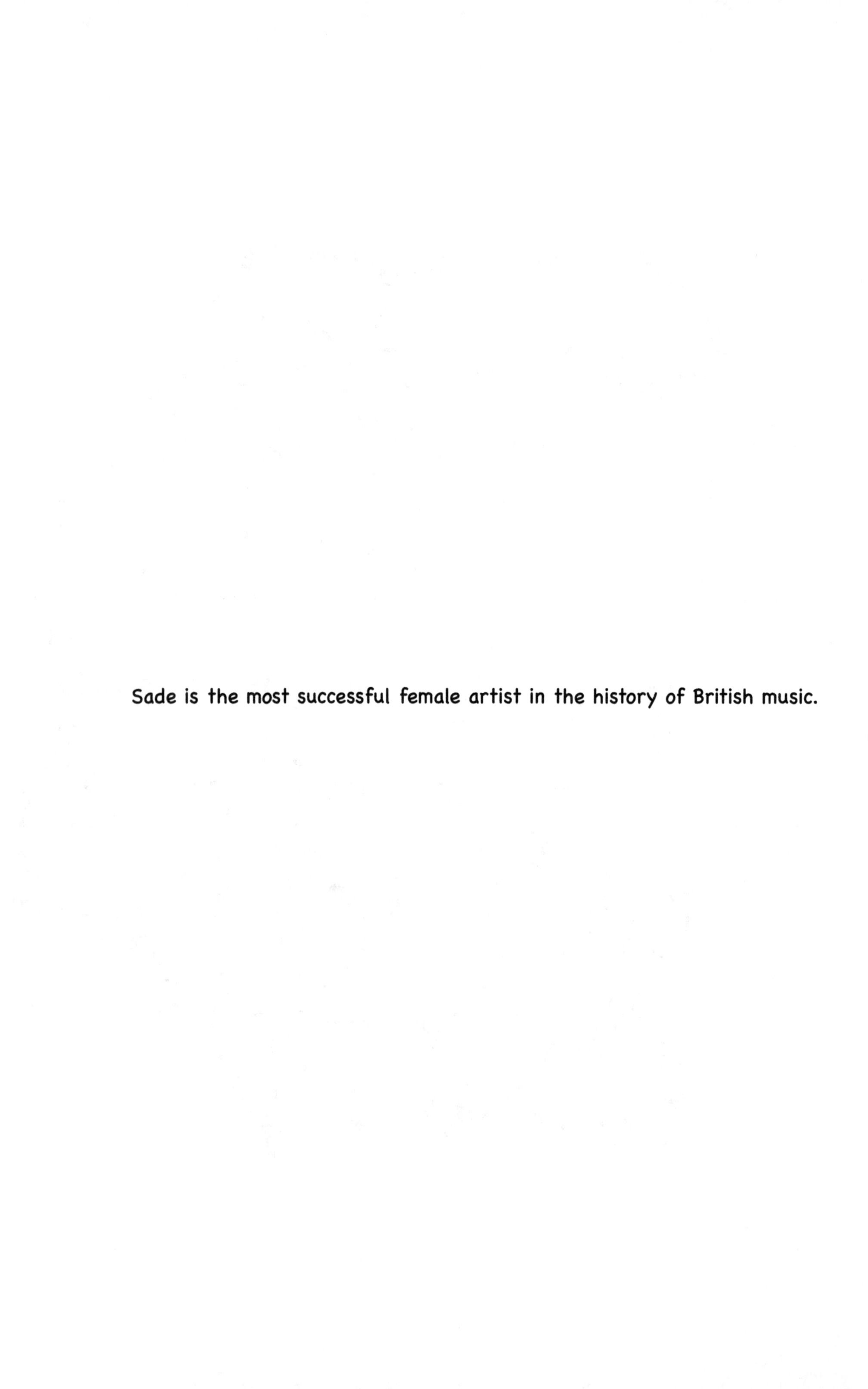
Sade is the most successful female artist in the history of British music.

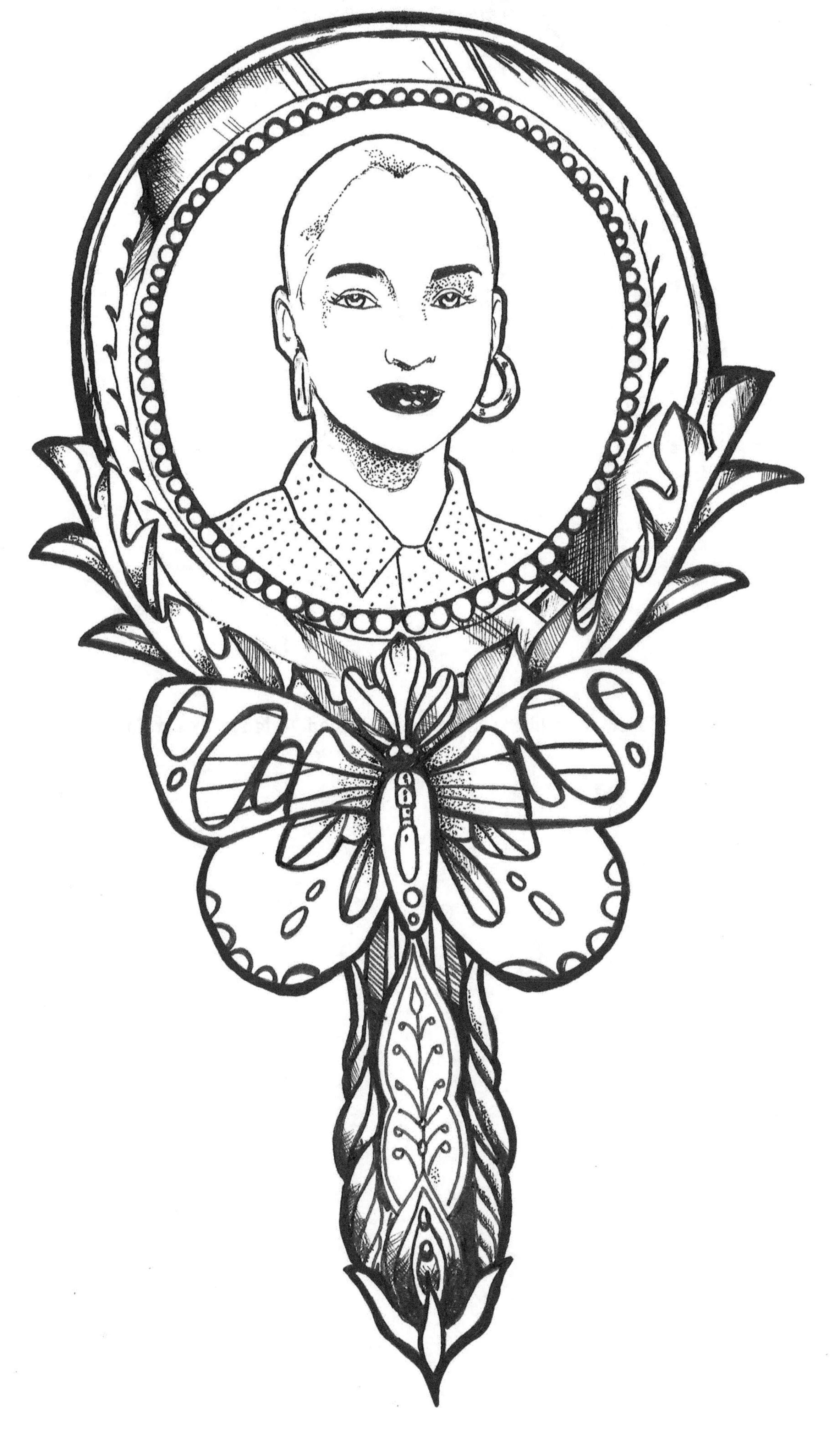

"I came in like a lamb, but I intend to leave like a lion."

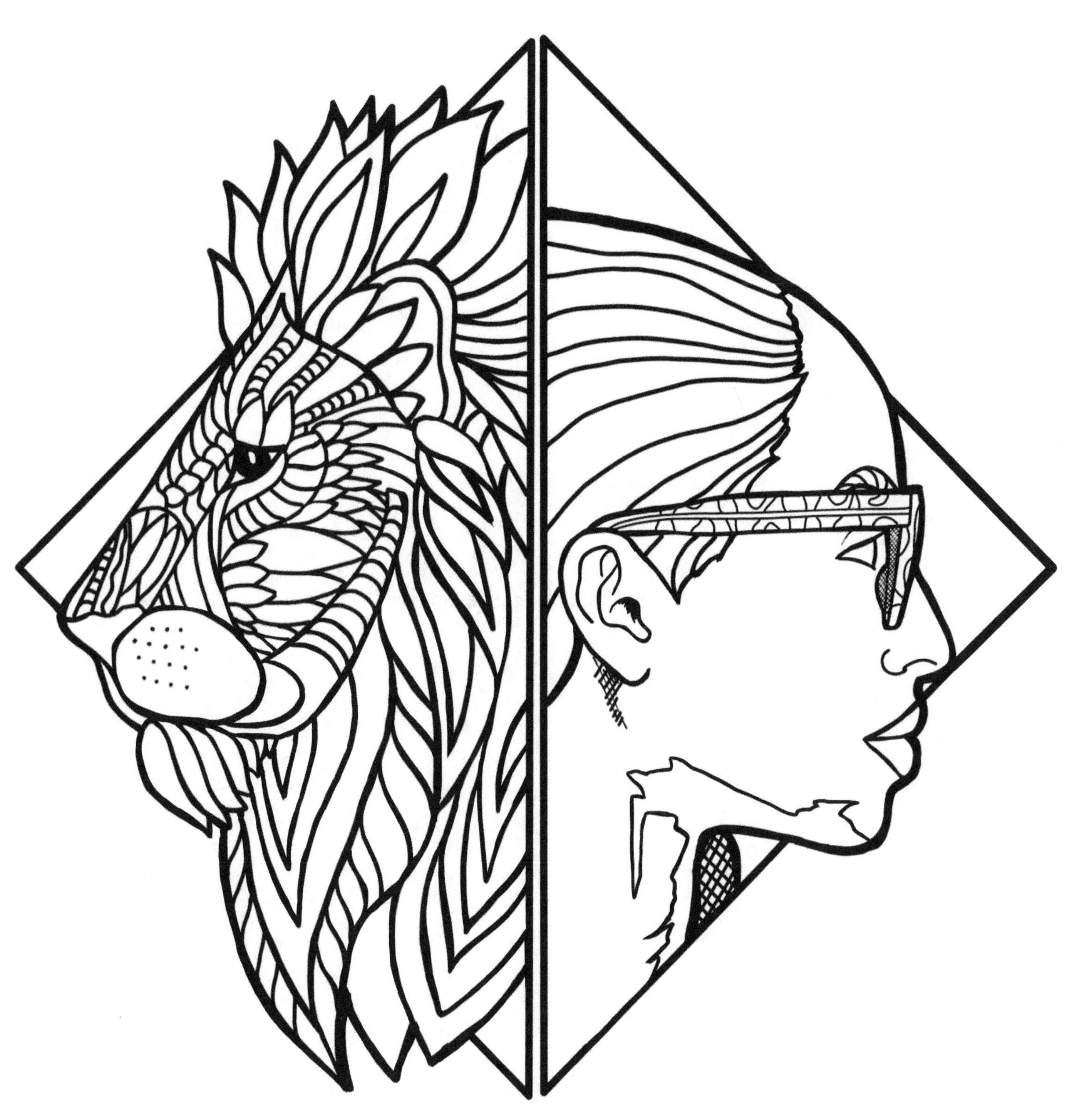

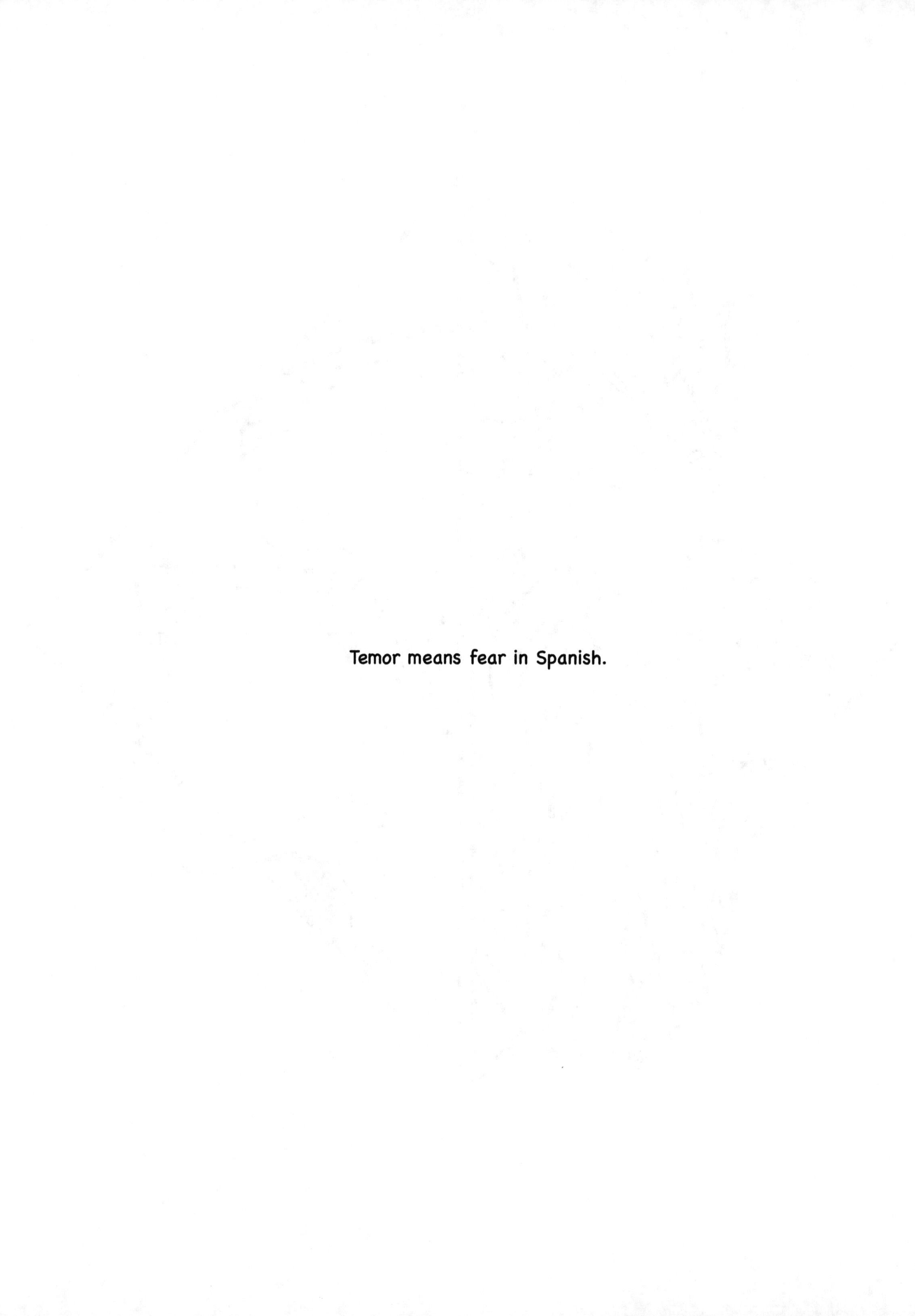

Temor means fear in Spanish.

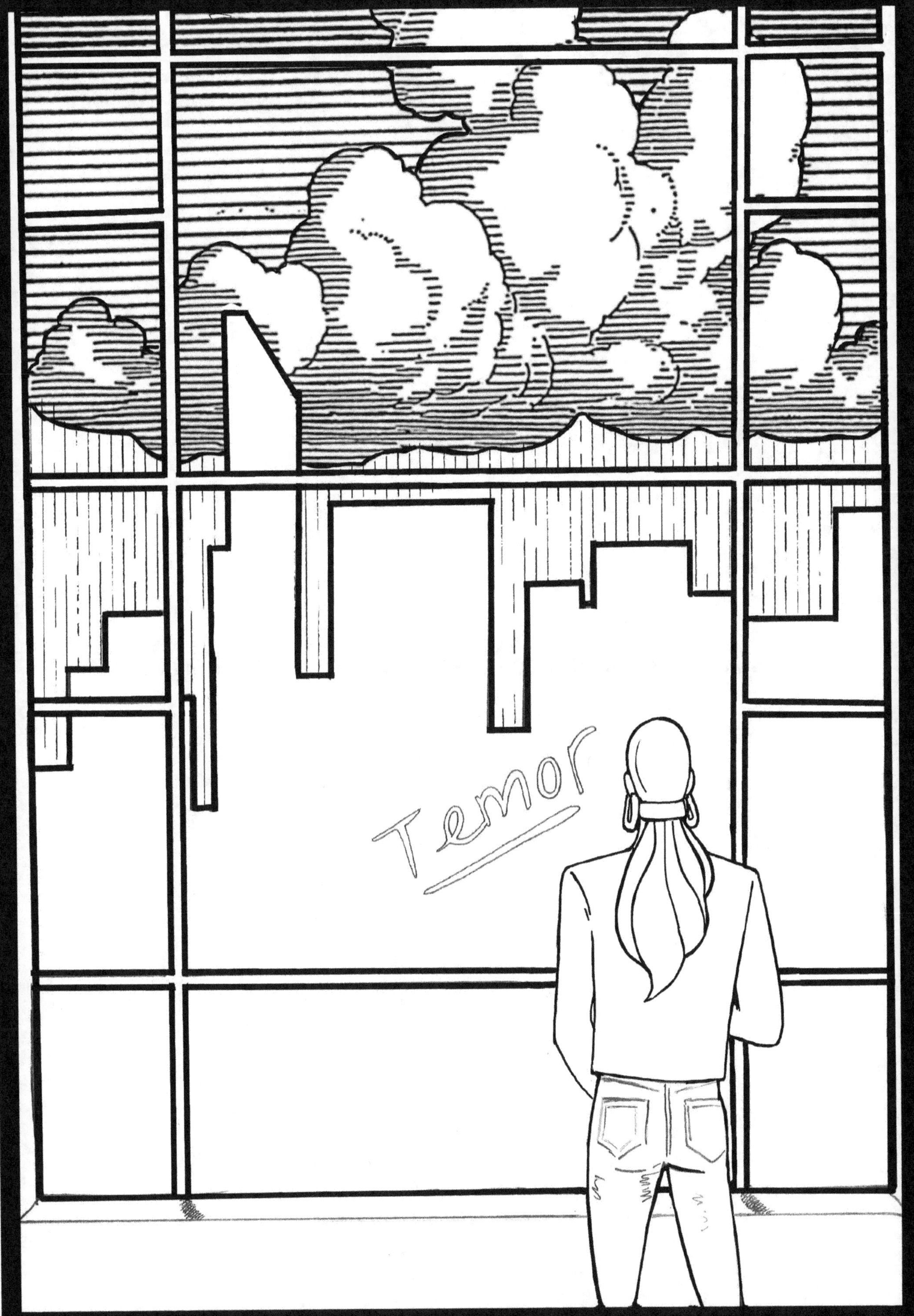
Temor

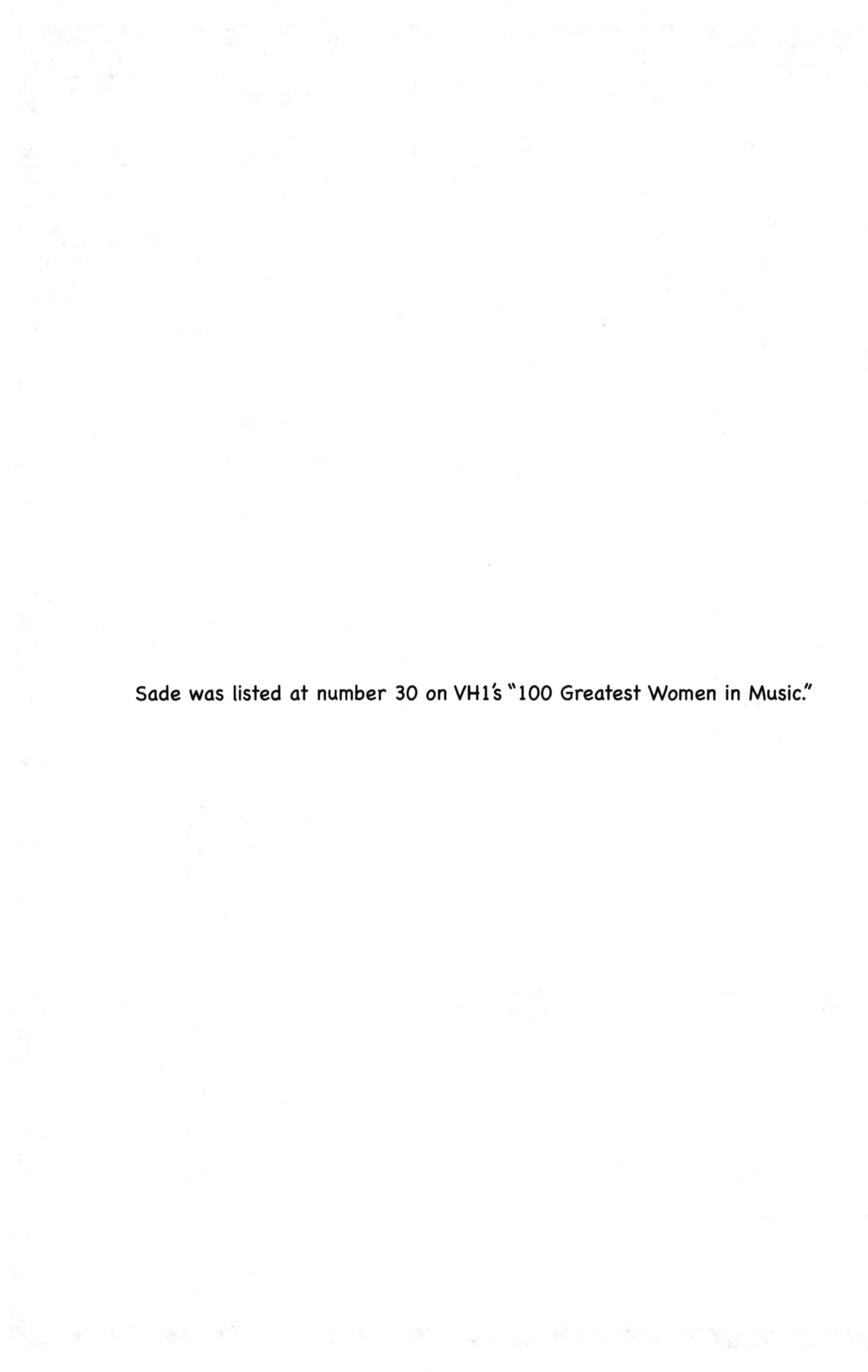

Sade was listed at number 30 on VH1's "100 Greatest Women in Music."

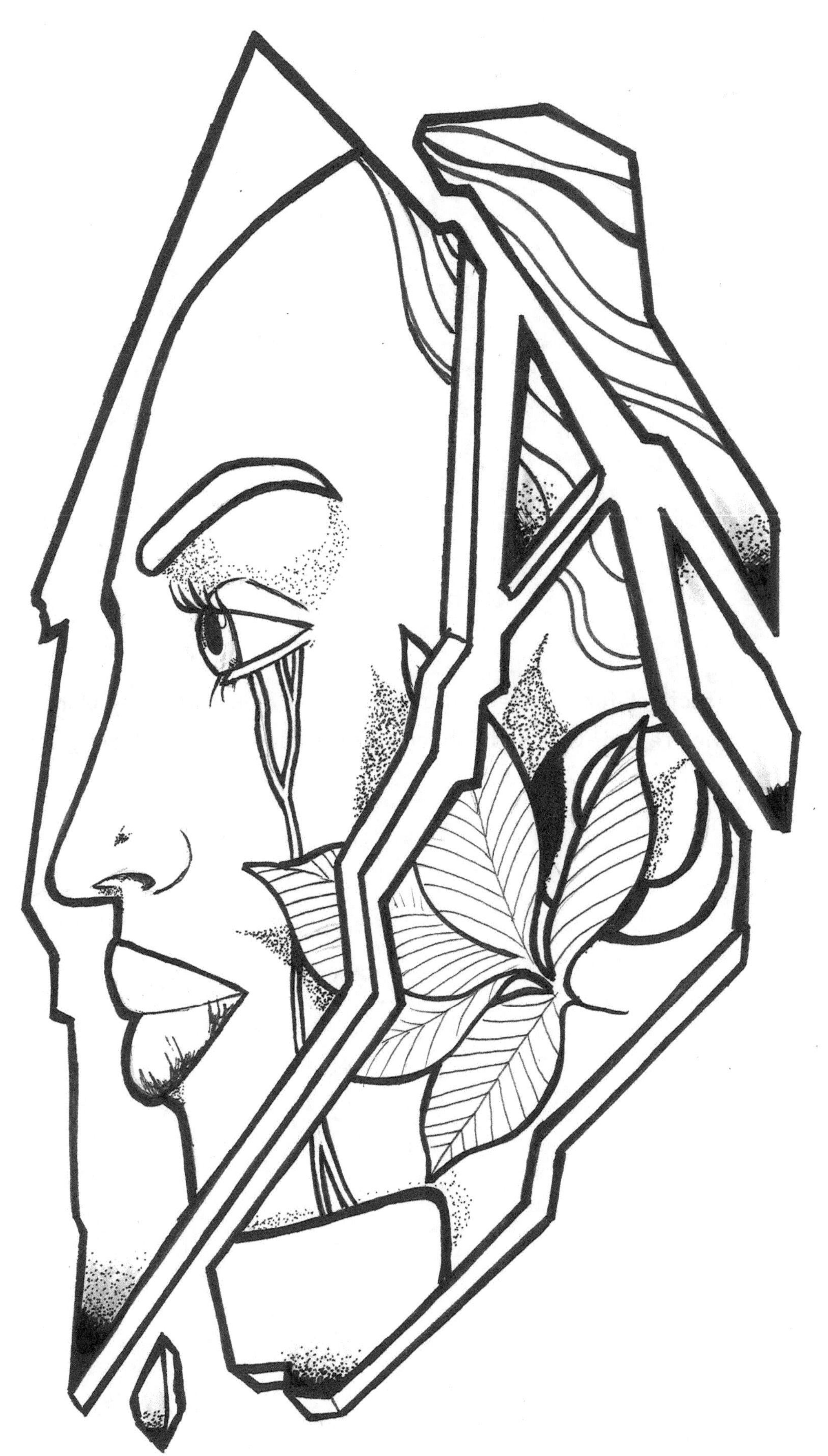

"The effects of fame were so dramatic that I didn't have any plans to make another record. If it hadn't been for the band, I would have given up."

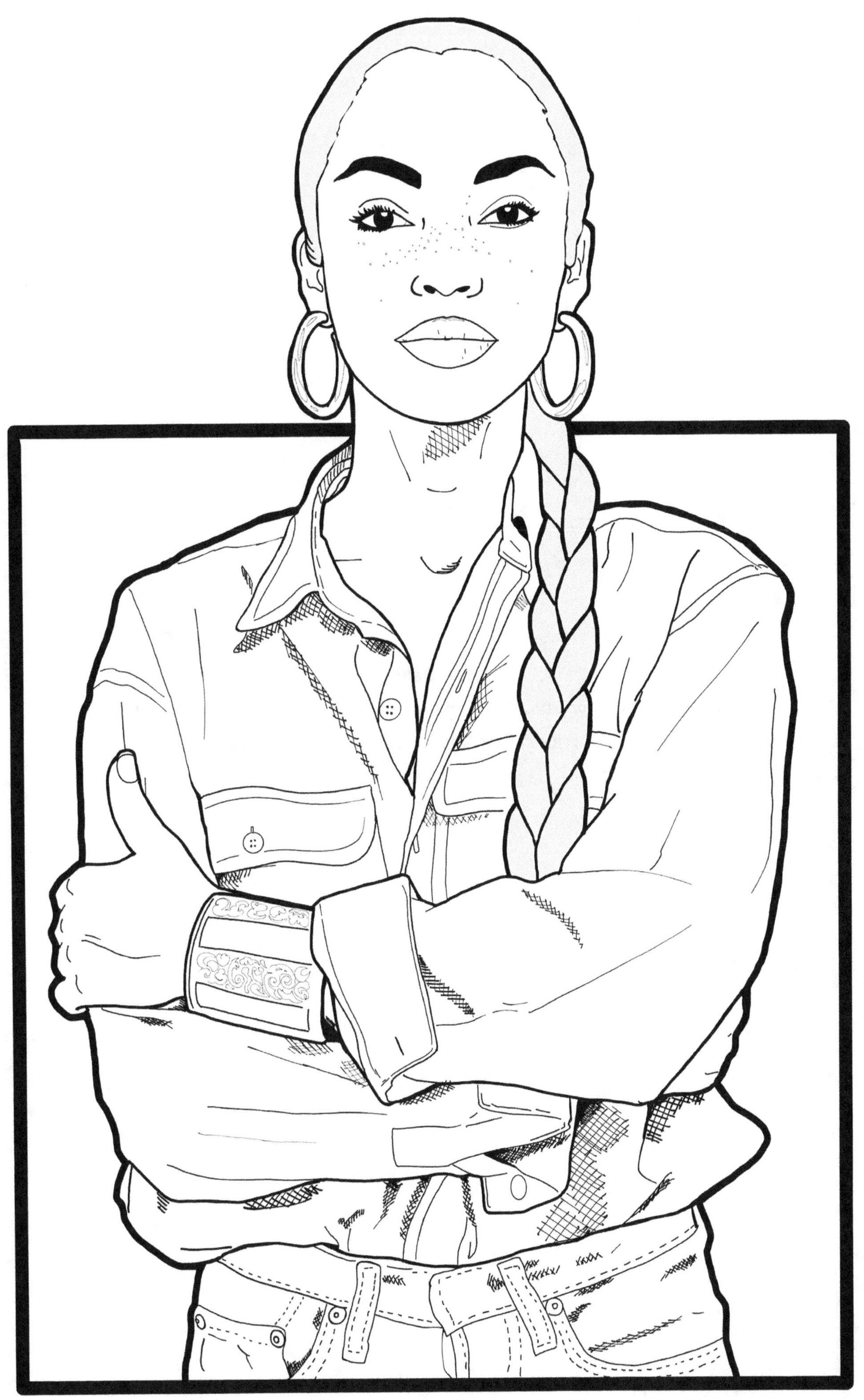

Love Deluxe

"One of the few luxury things you can't buy. You can buy any kind of love, but you can't get love deluxe."

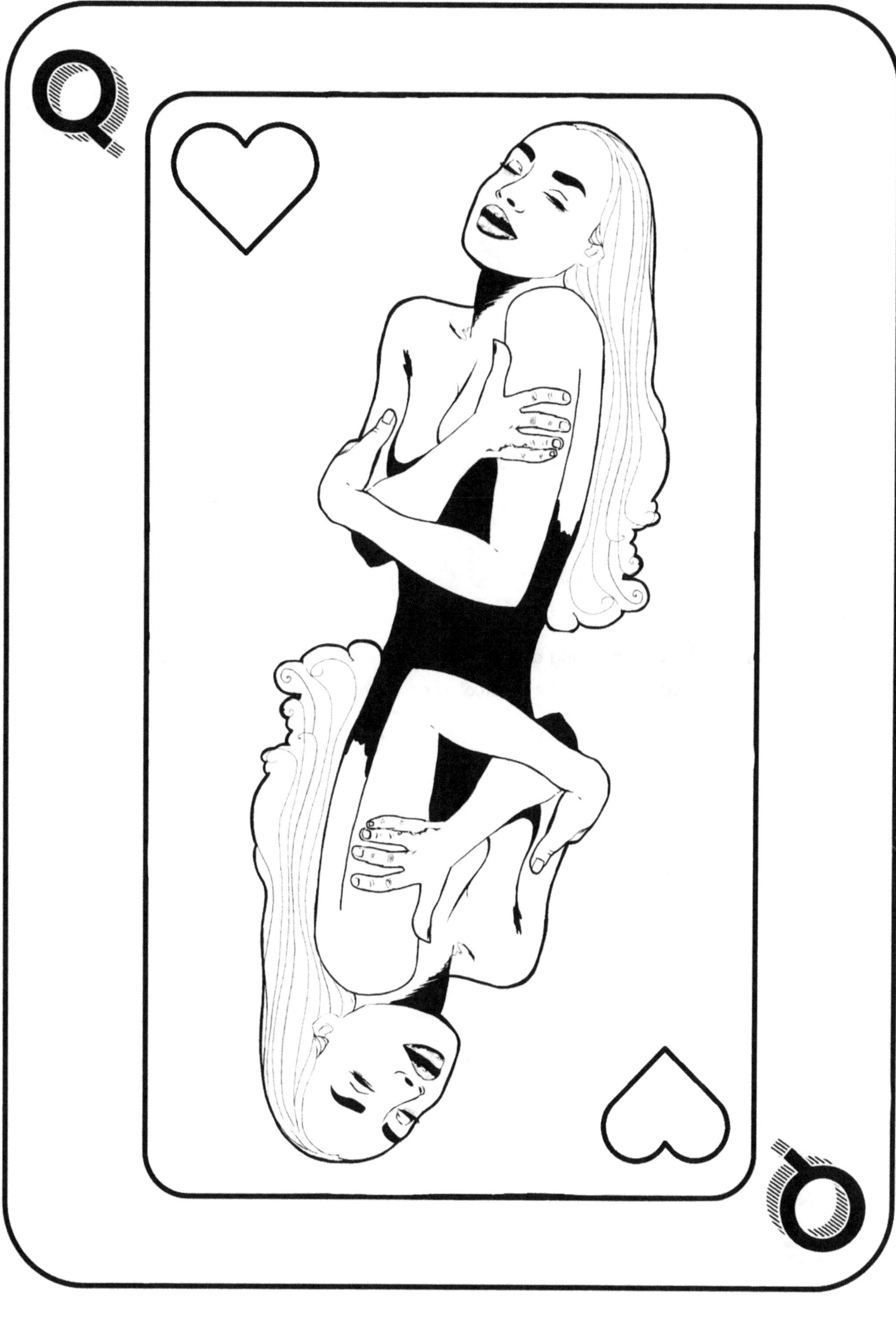
Q
Q

Sade made her acting debut in 1986 as Athene Duncannon alongside David Bowie in the musical rock movie "Absolute Beginners."

SADE

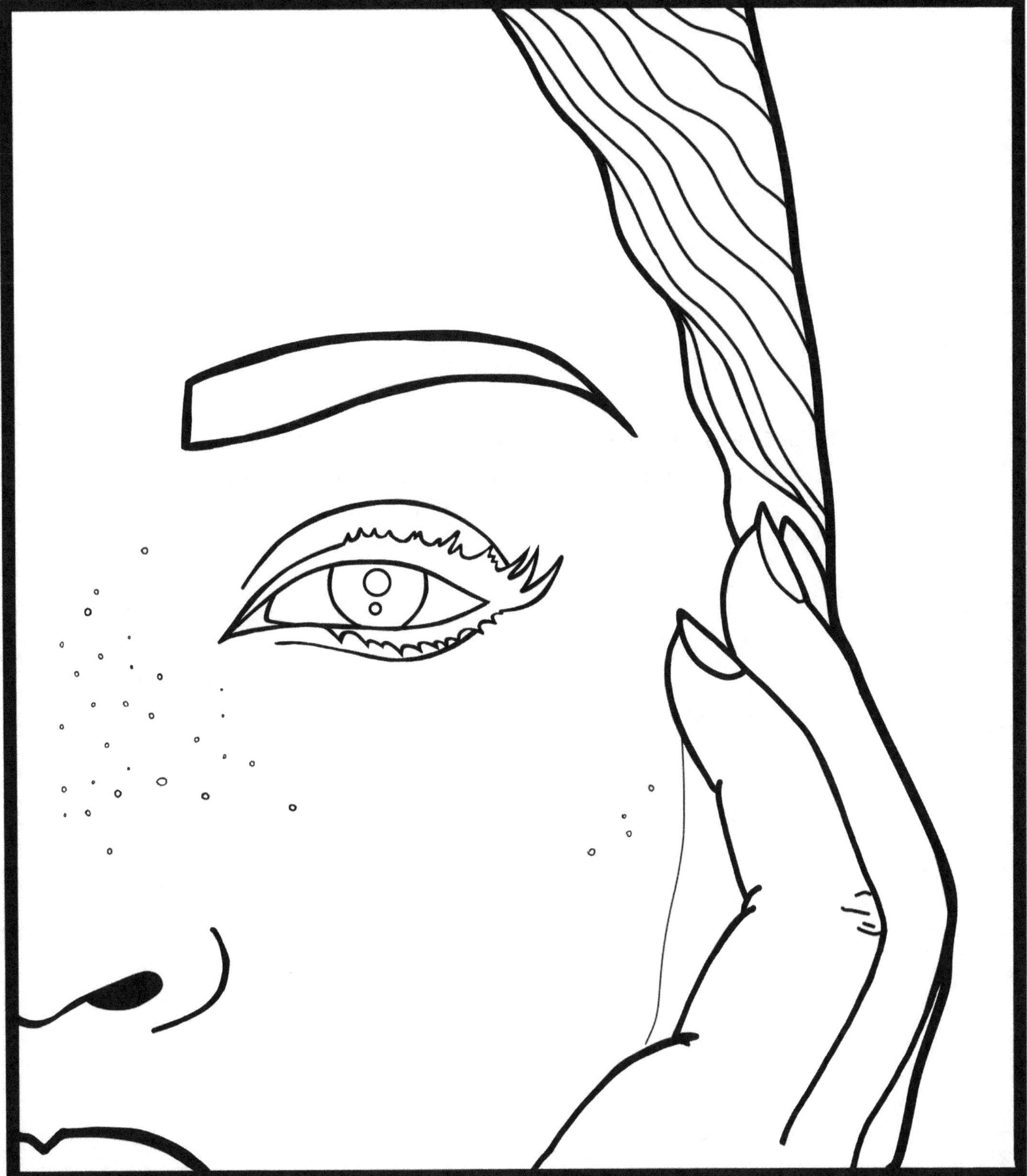

In 2002, Sade was named an officer of the Order of the British Empire. Prince Charles presented the award to her. Sade said she was accepting it on behalf of "all black women."

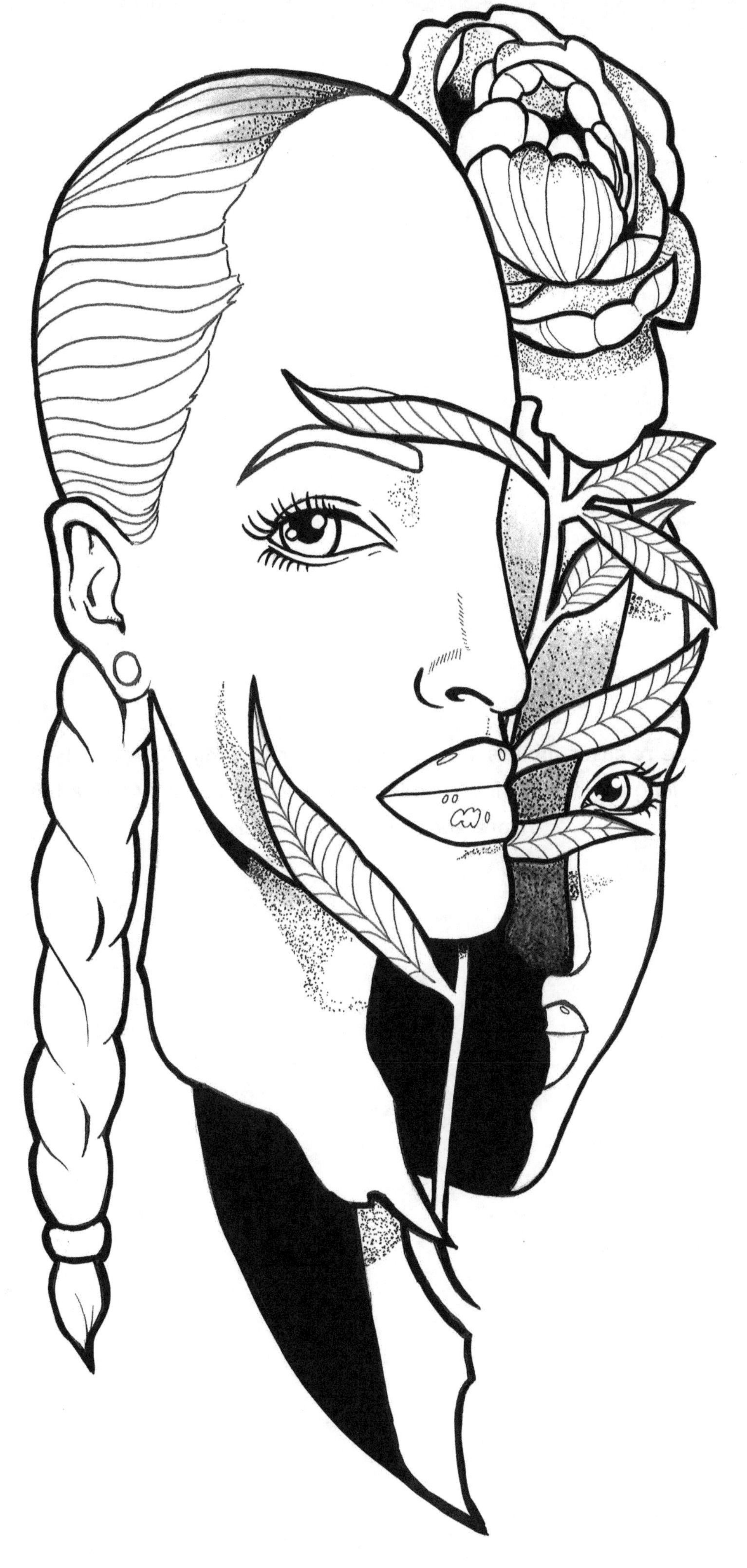

Sade releases albums very sporadically and is an expert at lying low for long periods of time. The lengthy breaks have only made her fans more eager for her reemergence.

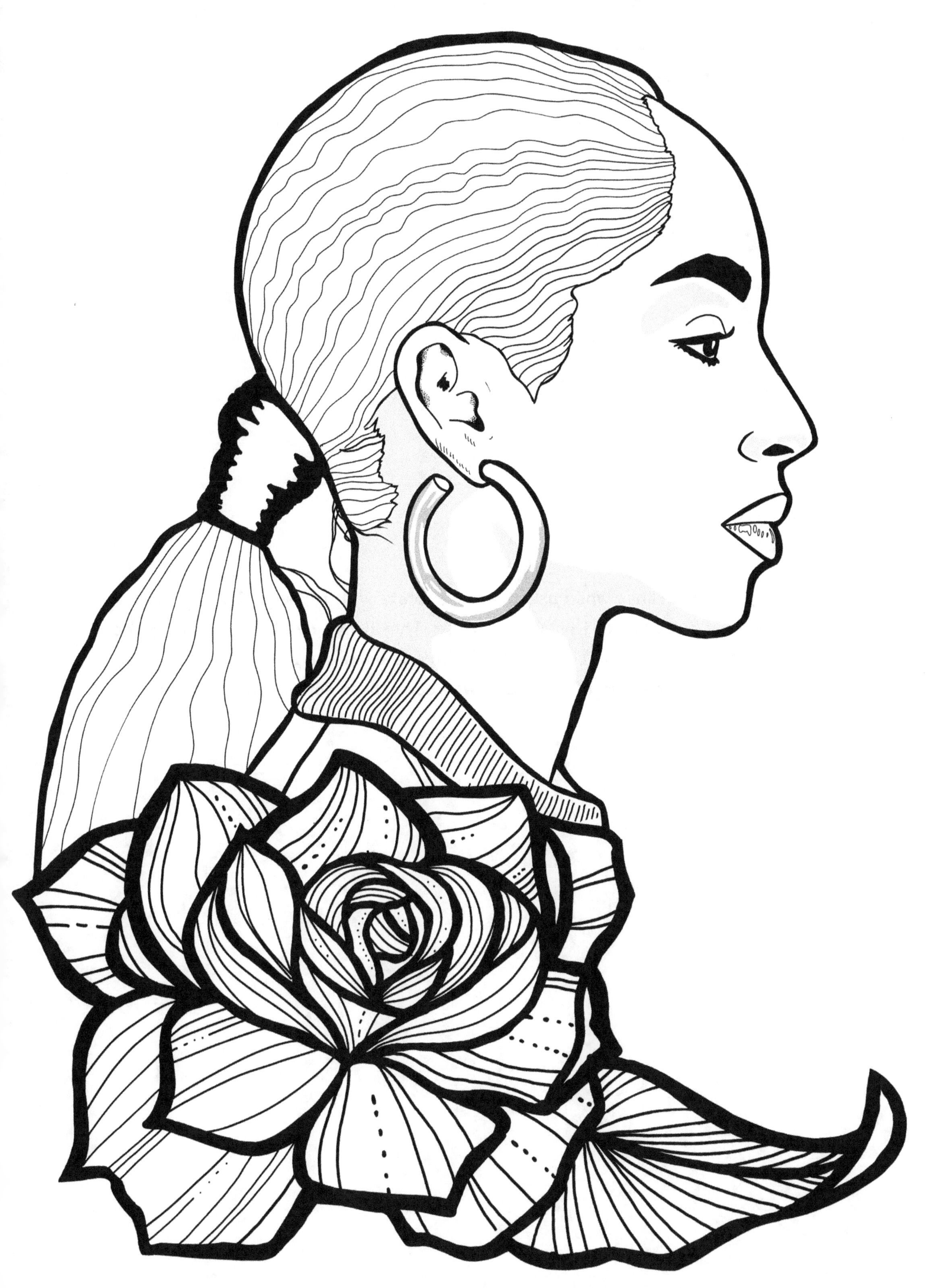

Sade politely declines when asked to collaborate with rappers. "I'm too scared they'll find me out. It's like The Wizard of Oz. They'll find out there's nothing there. As for collaborations, I'm collaborating with the band and do what we do. I see myself as a member of this band who does these songs that we write."

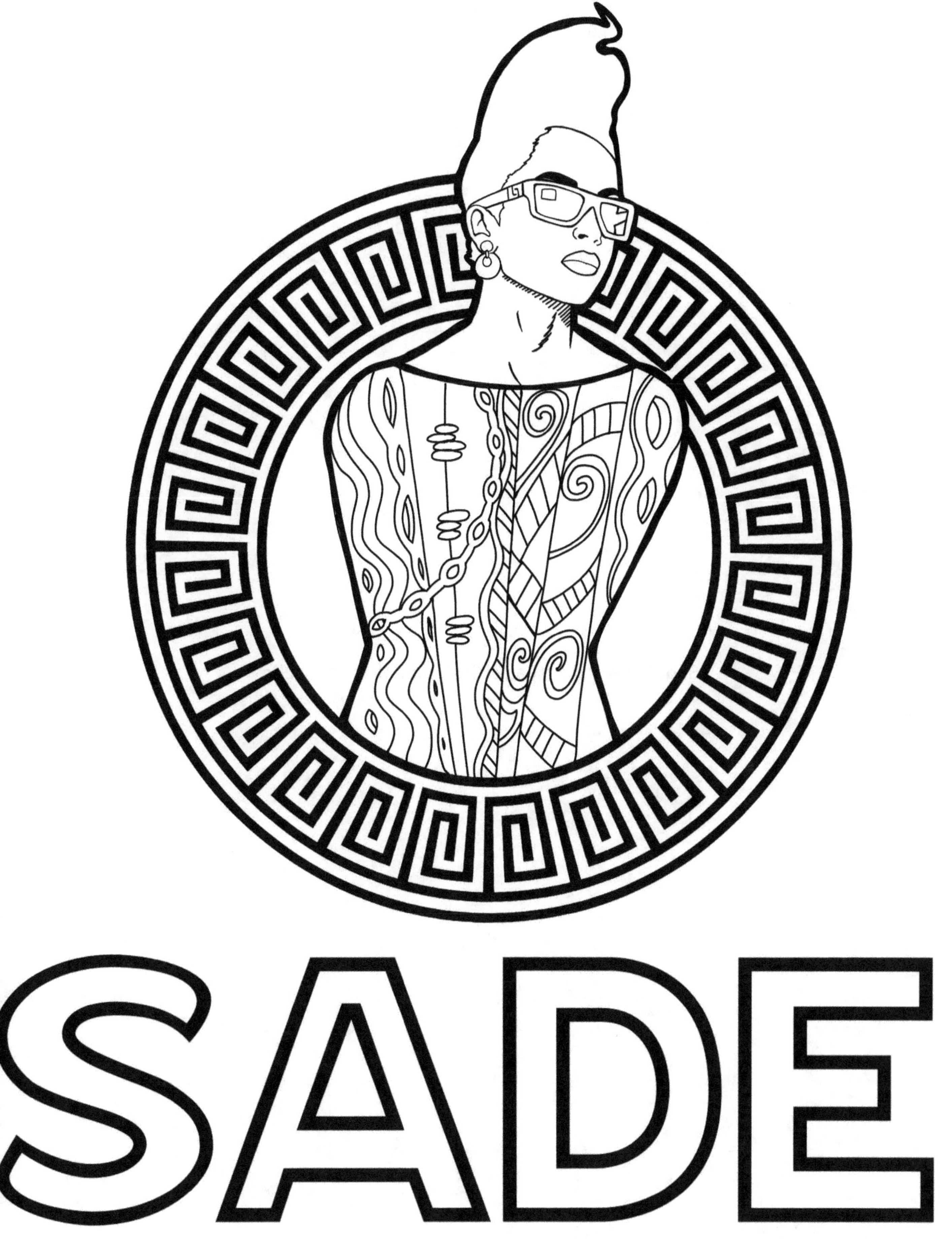

SADE

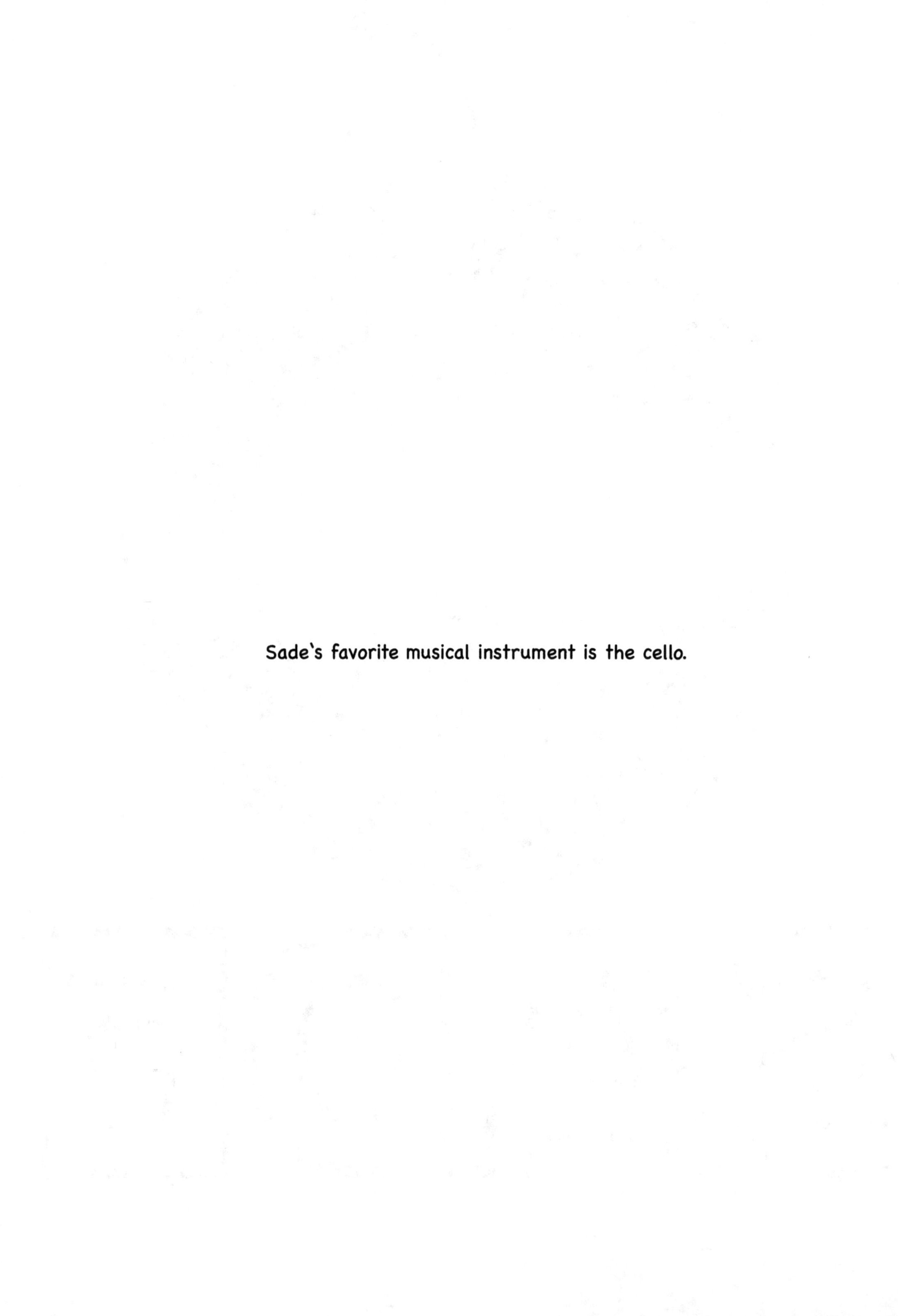

Sade's favorite musical instrument is the cello.

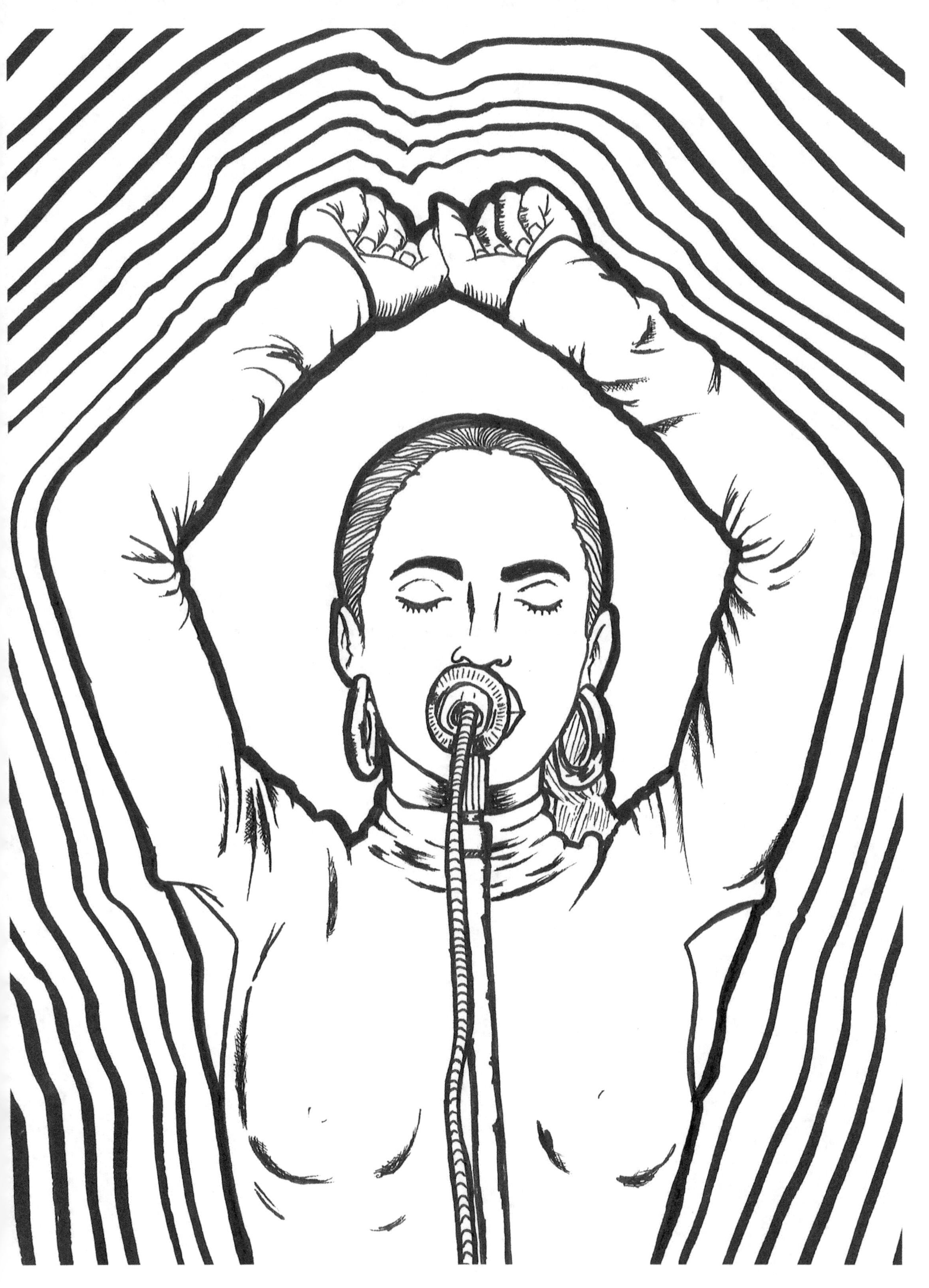

"You can only grow as an artist as long as you allow yourself the time to grow as a person."

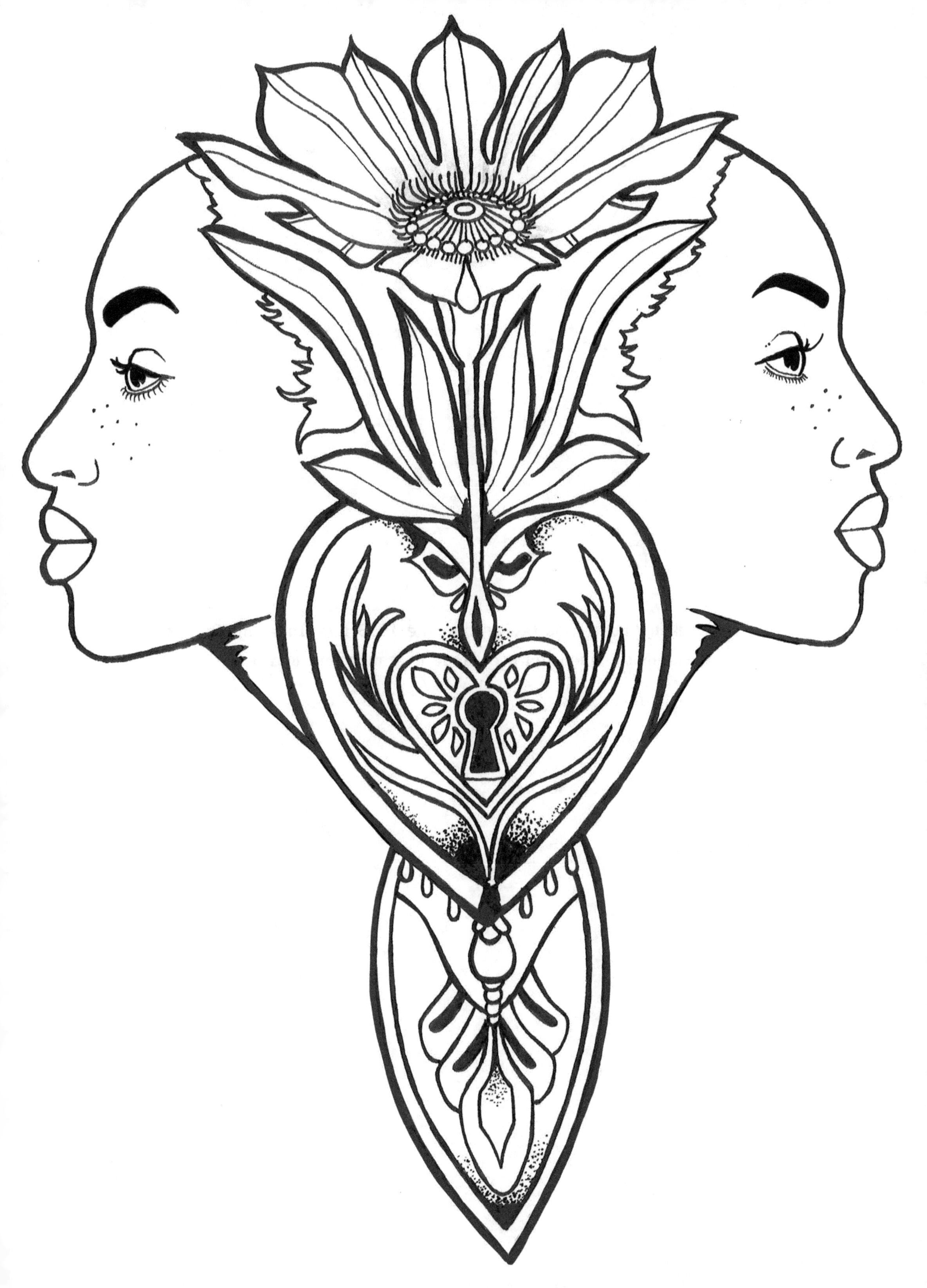

"No Ordinary Love" was featured in the 1993 film "Indecent Proposal." The music video features Sade as a mermaid and a bride.

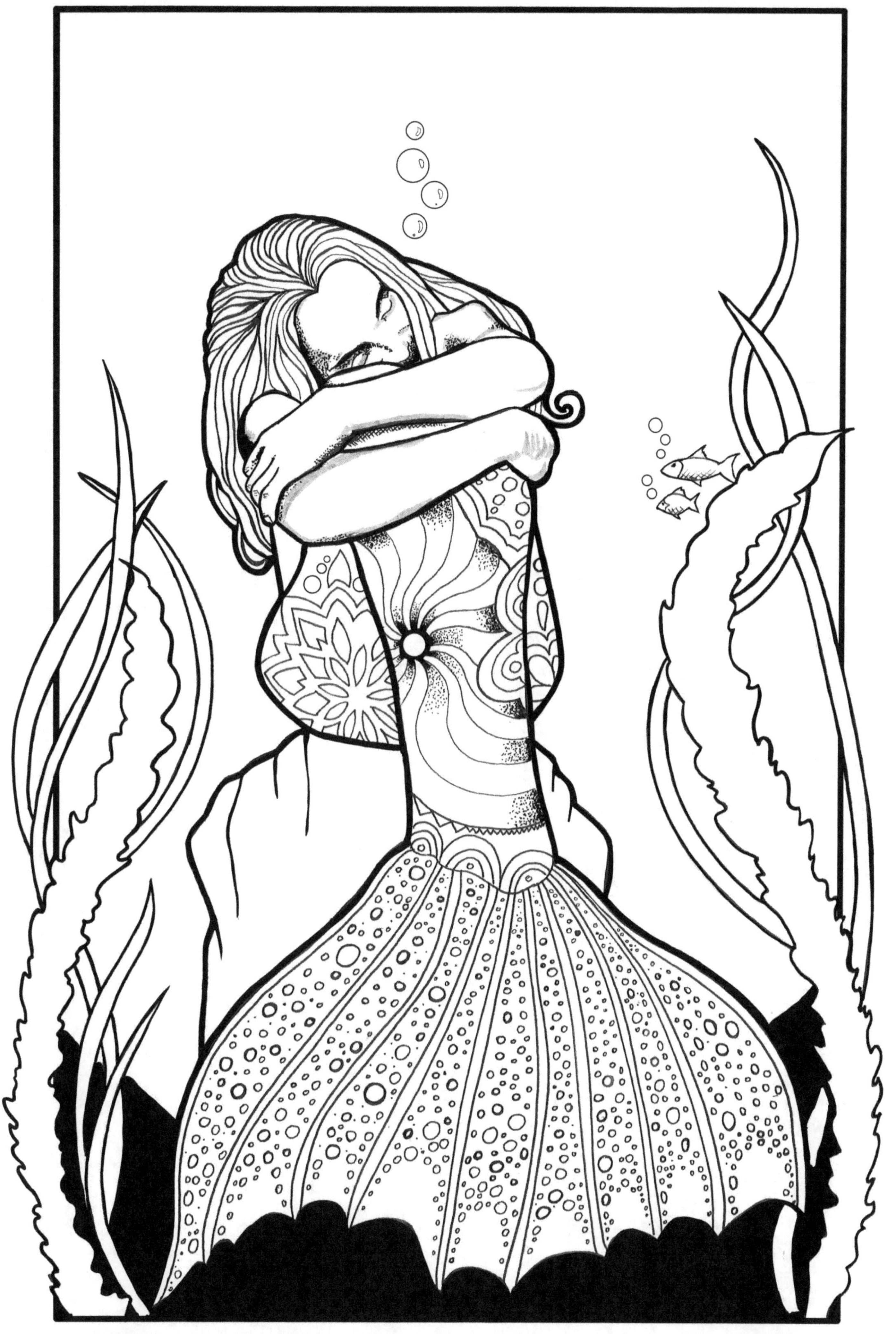

"Cherish the Day" was shot on a Manhattan rooftop.

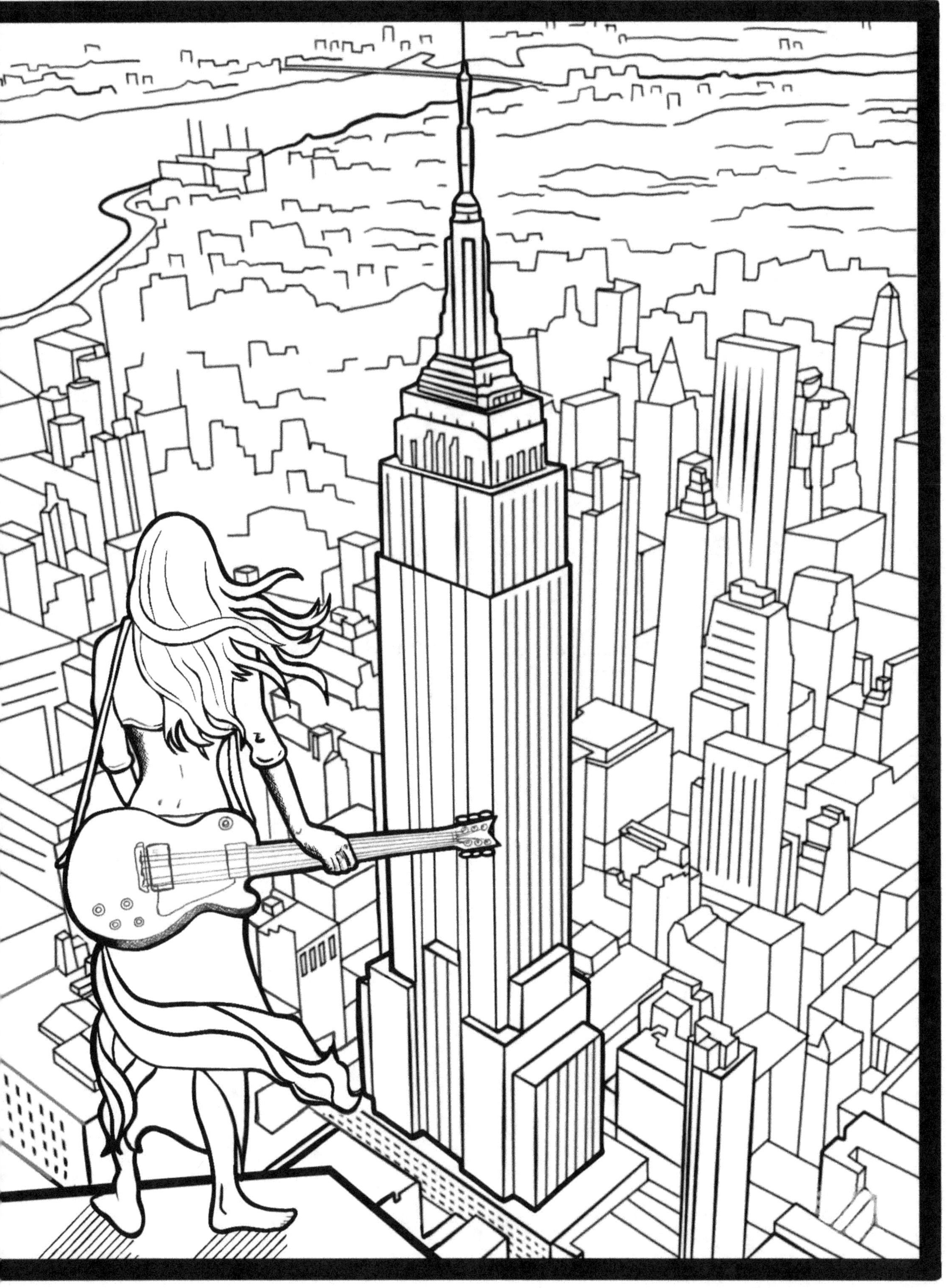

The Best of Sade was released in 1994.

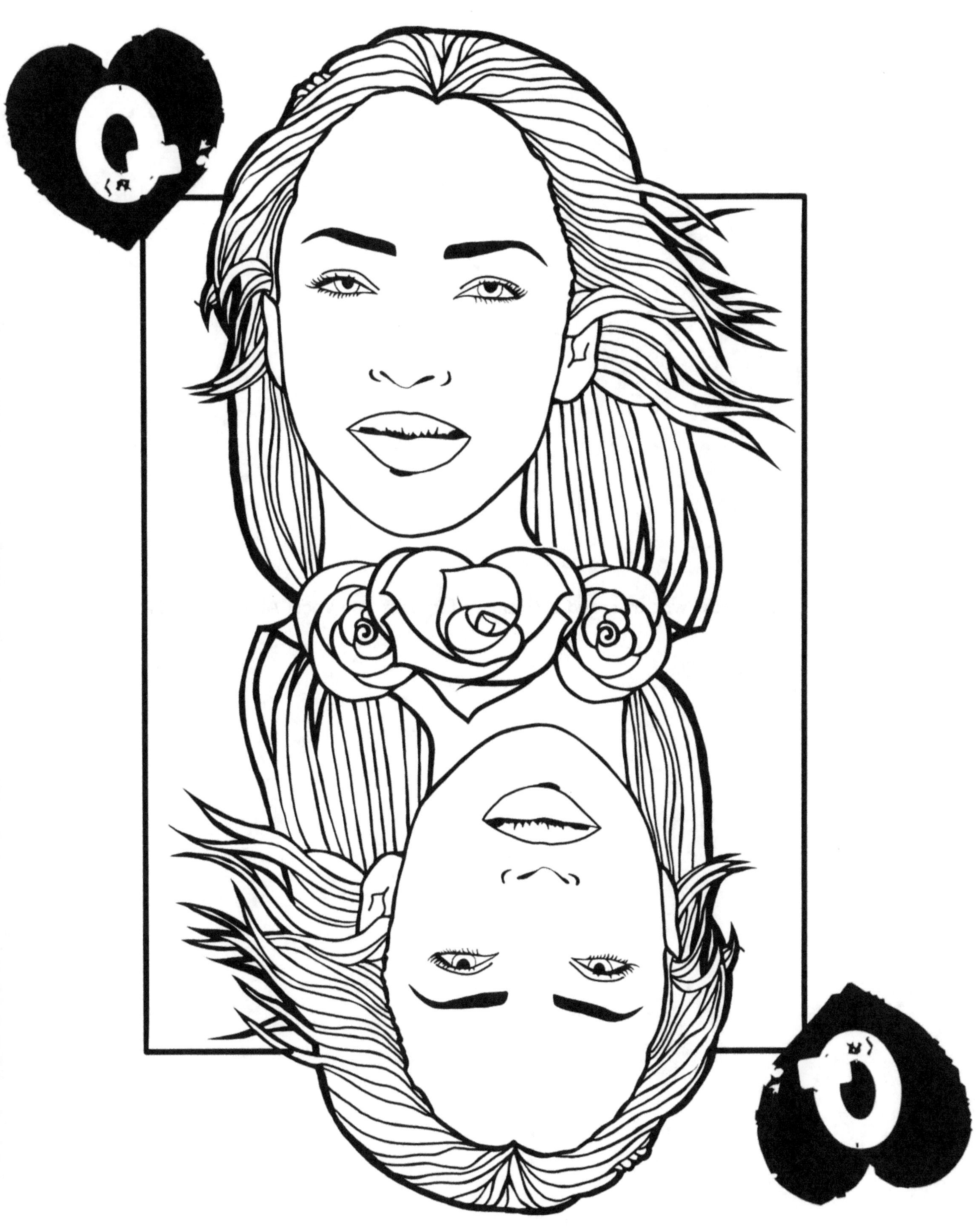

"Lovers Rock" was awarded a Grammy for Best Pop Vocal Album in 2002.

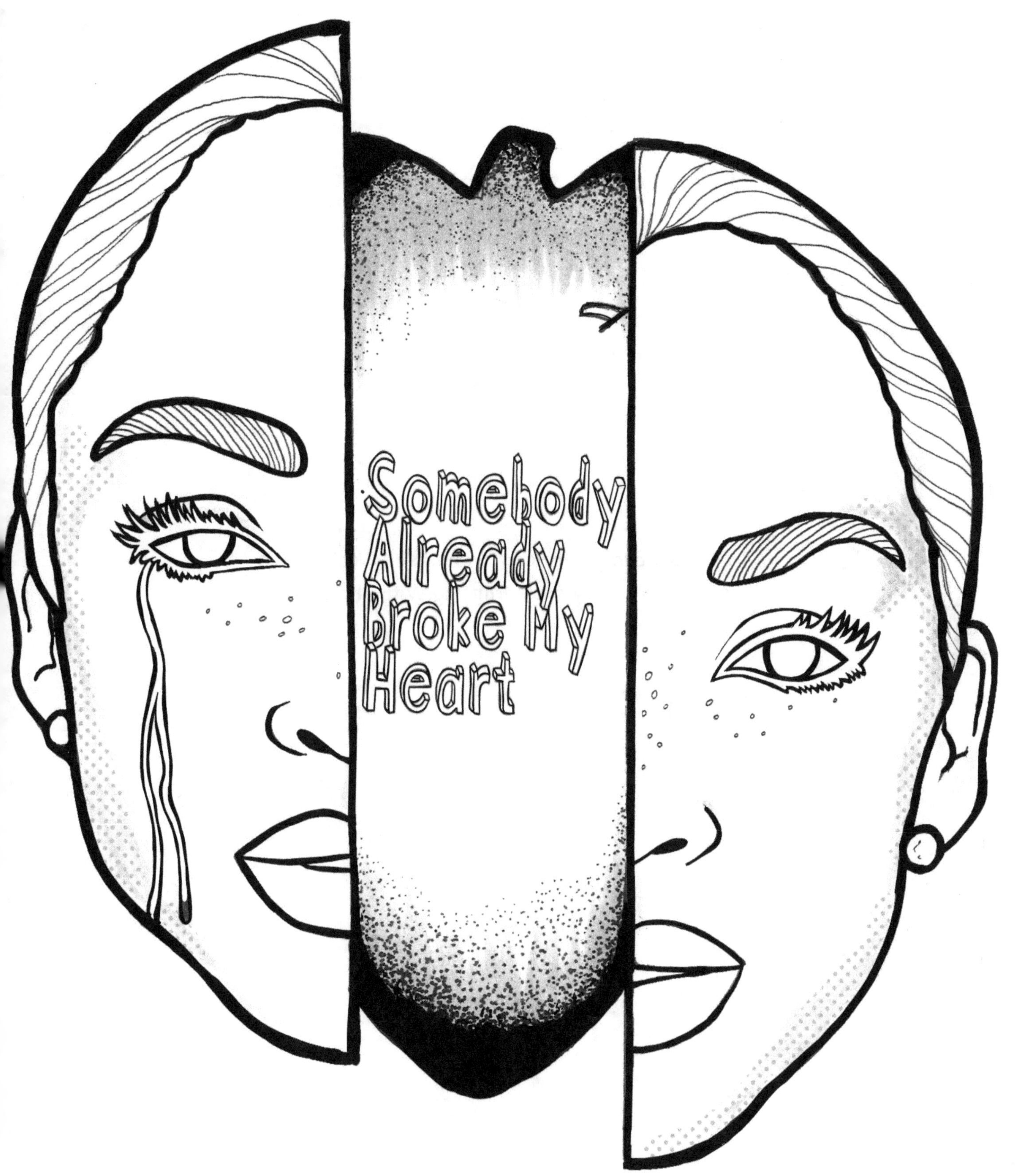
Somebody
Already
Broke My
Heart

In 2010, Sade performed "Sweetest Taboo" on the American reality show Dancing With the Stars.

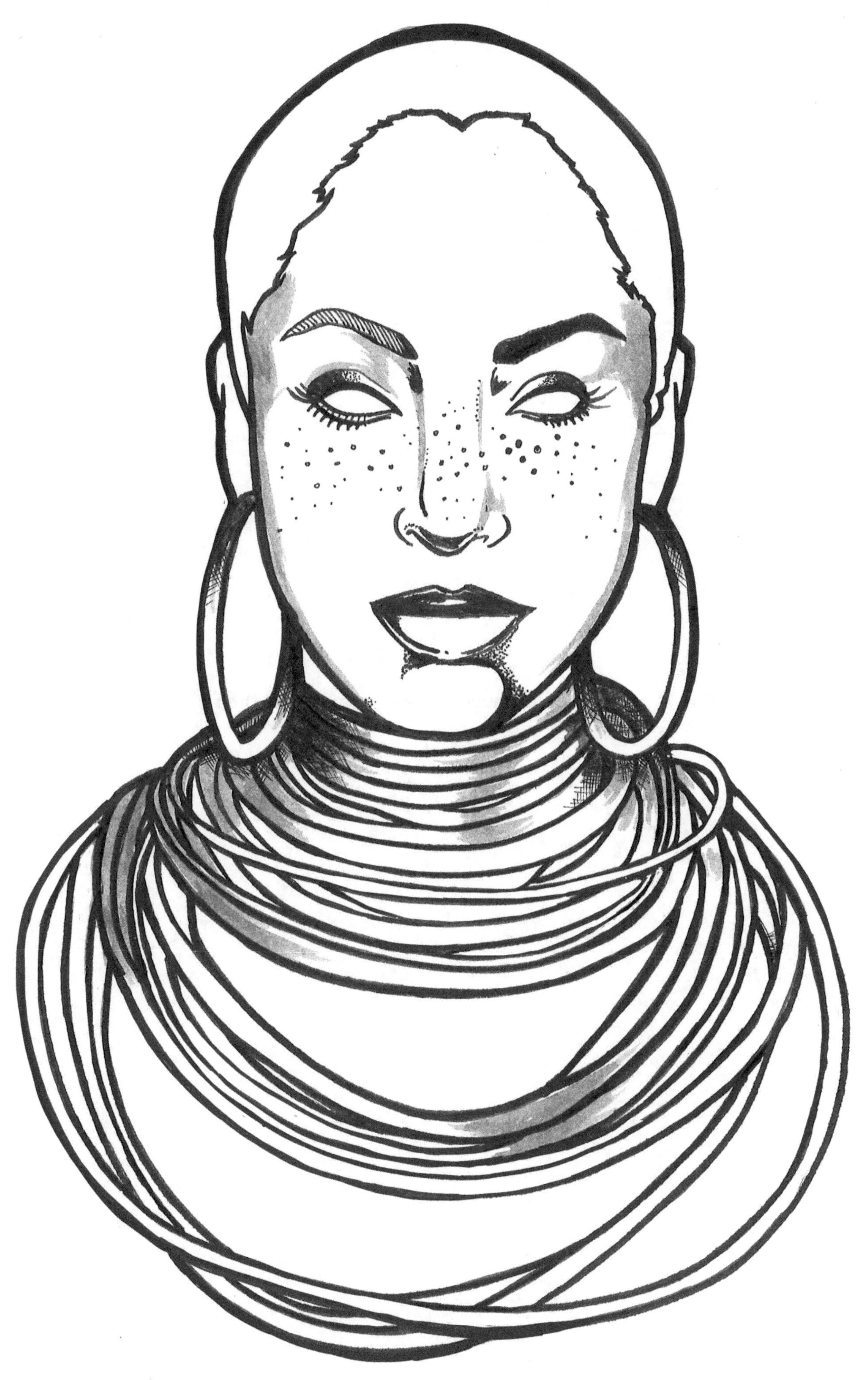

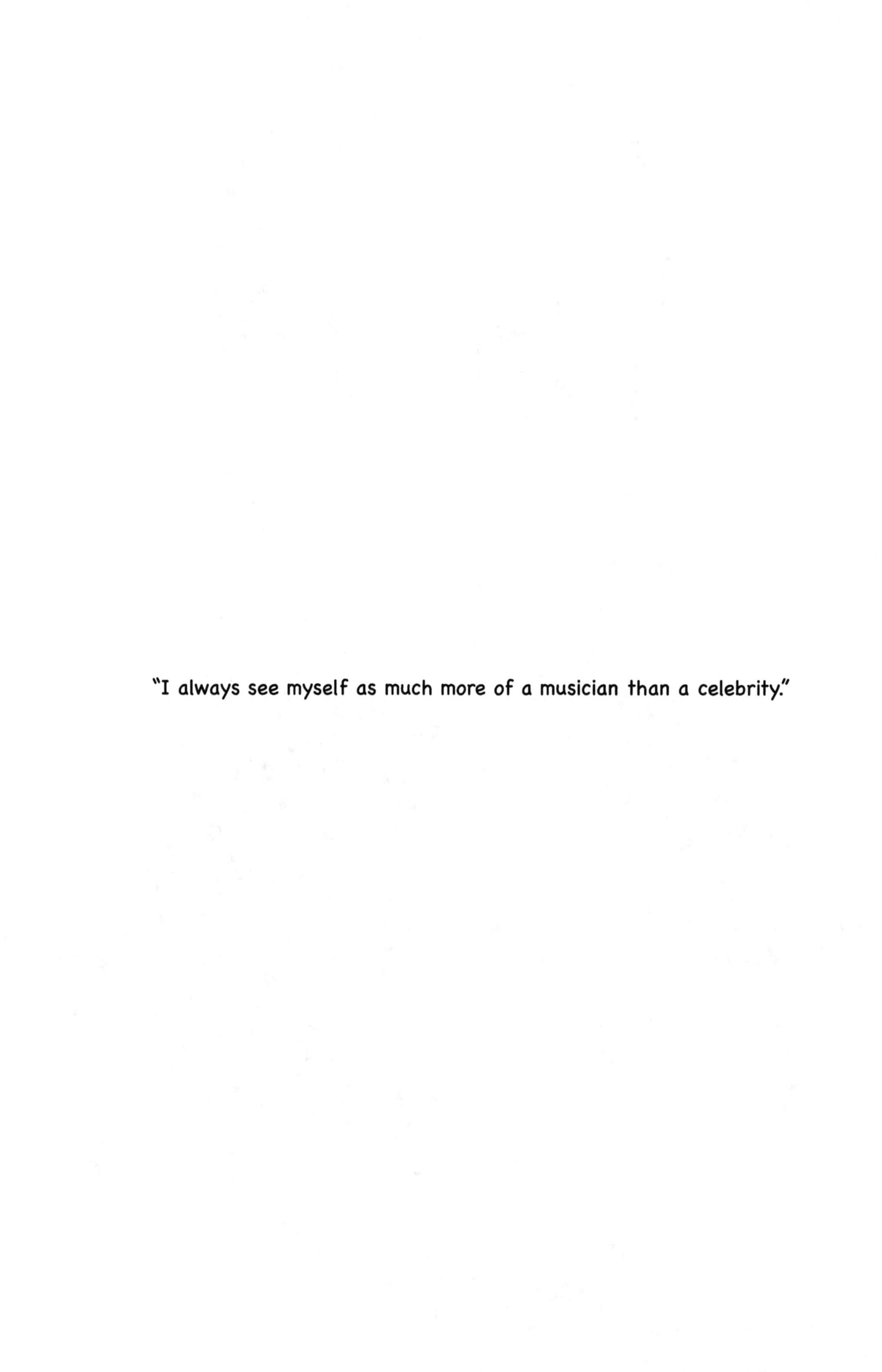

"I always see myself as much more of a musician than a celebrity."

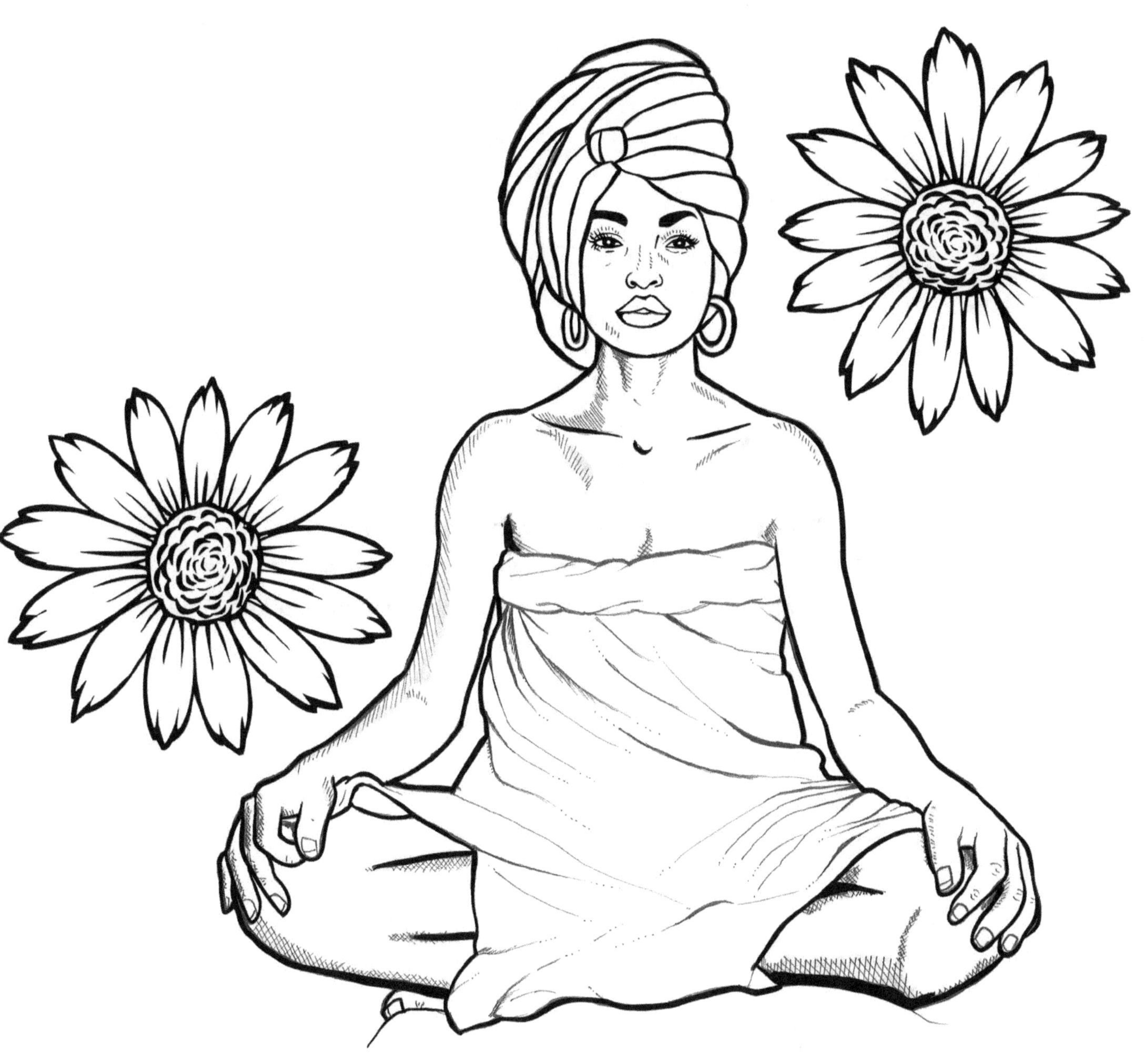

"I don't think I'm so sultry and mysterious.
I just don't want people to have too much of me.
I put a lot of myself into the music, and that's how you get to know me."

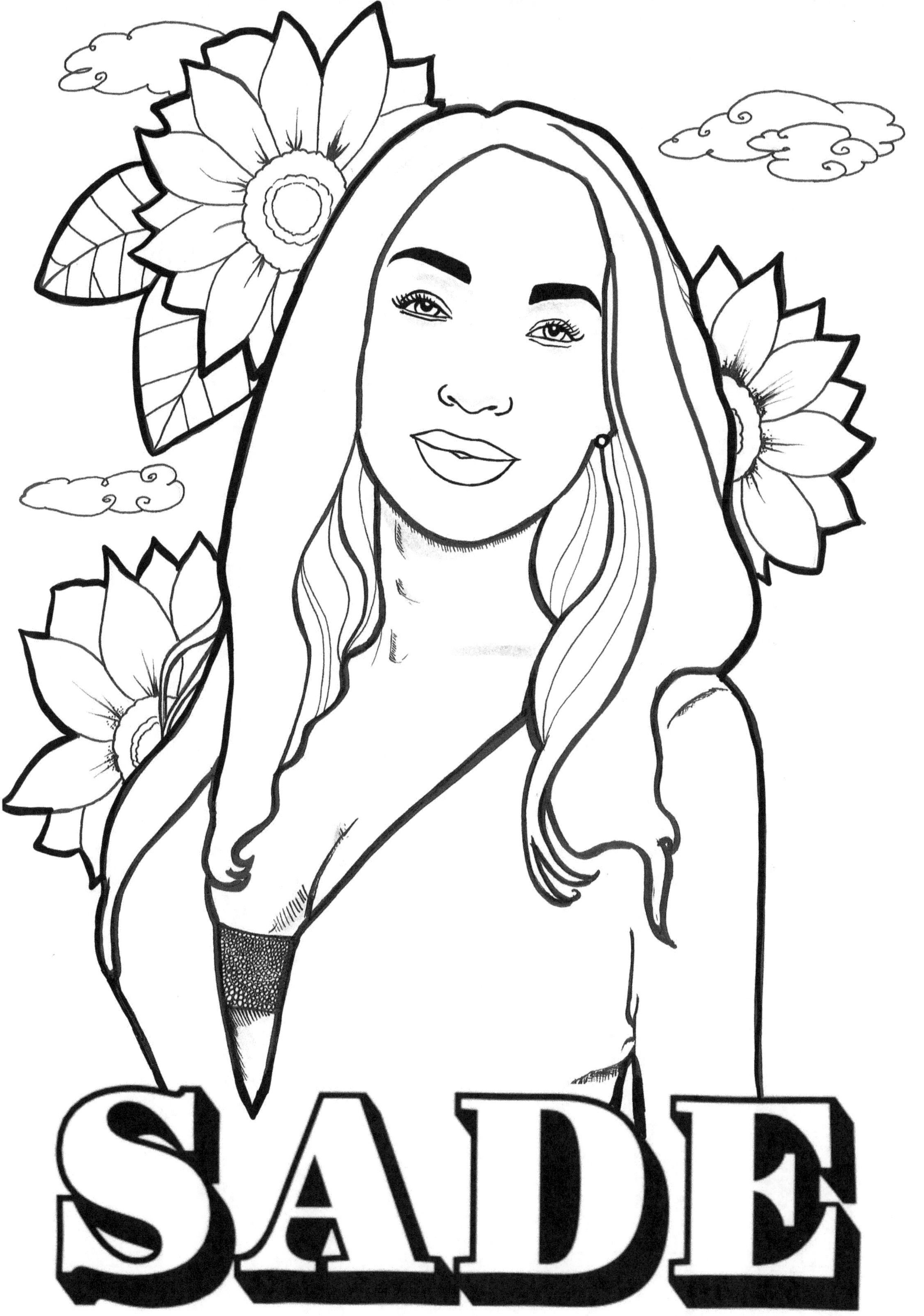
SADE

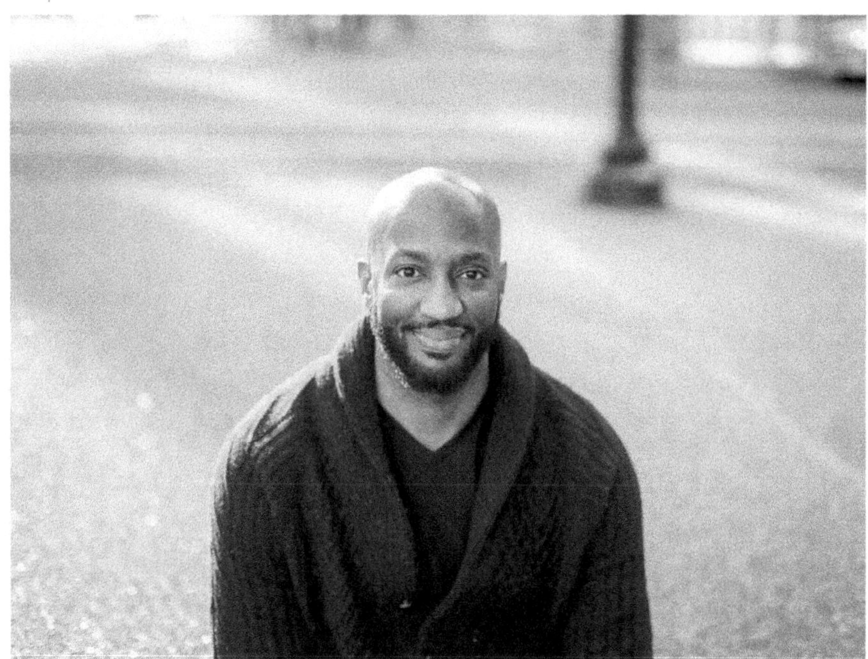

Andre Hollingsworth is a self-taught artist from Sierra Vista, Arizona. When he was a child, his mother quickly learned that he loved coloring books. He entertained himself for hours with the ample supply of coloring books she kept at home. As Andre grew older, he became interested in comic books and began experimenting with drawing some of his favorite superheroes in his sketchbook.

Andre is committed to ensuring that art is accessible to the community in a variety of ways. His most recent project, a series of coloring books, offers adults and children an artistic activity that is both creative and soothing. Andre is highly motivated to produce work that will empower young people to imagine breaking barriers in sports, music, and other industries.

Through his artwork, Andre hopes to inspire young people not only to tap into their artistic creativity, but also to appreciate the continuing influence in renowned Black artists on today's musical landscape.

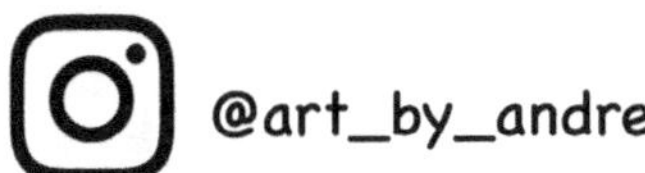
@art_by_andre

Art By Andre Hollingsworth

www.ingramcontent.com/pod-product-compliance
Lightning Source LLC
LaVergne TN
LVHW061256100826
845148LV00008B/1151
* 9 7 8 1 7 3 5 2 1 7 7 0 3 *